Shakespeare in the Theatre: Tina Packer

SHAKESPEARE IN THE THEATRE

SERIES EDITORS
Peter Holland, Farah Karim-Cooper and Stephen Purcell

Published titles

Nicholas Hytner, Abigail Rokison-Woodall
The American Shakespeare Center, Paul Menzer
Mark Rylance at the Globe, Stephen Purcell
Patrice Chéreau, Dominique Goy-Blanquet
Peter Sellars, Ayanna Thompson
The National Theatre, 1963–1975: Olivier and Hall,
Robert Shaughnessy
Trevor Nunn, Russell Jackson
Cheek by Jowl, Peter Kirwan
Peter Hall, Stuart Hampton-Reeves
Yukio Ninagawa, Conor Hanratty
The King's Men, Lucy Munro
Sir William Davenant and the Duke's Company, Amanda
Eubanks Winkler and Richard Schoch
Sarah Siddons and John Philip Kemble, Fiona Ritchie
The Stratford Festival, Christie Carson

Forthcoming

Shakespeare Theatre Company, Drew Lichtenberg and
Deborah C. Payne
Satoshi Miyagi, Mika Eglinton
Phyllida Lloyd, Elizabeth Schafer
Kathryn Hunter, Stephen Purcell
Reduced Shakespeare Company, Ronan Hatfull

Shakespeare in the Theatre: Tina Packer

Katharine Goodland

THE ARDEN SHAKESPEARE
LONDON • NEW YORK • OXFORD • NEW DELHI • SYDNEY

THE ARDEN SHAKESPEARE
Bloomsbury Publishing Plc, 50 Bedford Square, London, WC1B 3DP, UK
Bloomsbury Publishing Inc, 1359 Broadway, 12th Floor, New York, NY 10018, USA
Bloomsbury Publishing Ireland, 29 Earlsfort Terrace, Dublin 2, D02 AY28, Ireland

BLOOMSBURY, THE ARDEN SHAKESPEARE and the Arden Shakespeare logo are trademarks of Bloomsbury Publishing Plc

First published in Great Britain 2024
This paperback edition published 2026

Copyright © Katharine Goodland, 2024

Katharine Goodland has asserted her right under the Copyright, Designs and Patents Act, 1988, to be identified as author of this work.

For legal purposes the Acknowledgements on p. viii constitute an extension of this copyright page.

Series design by Dani Leigh
Cover image: *A Midsummer Night's Dream*. Directed by Tina Packer at the The Mount, Lenox, MA (2001) (Photo © Kevin Sprague)

All rights reserved. No part of this publication may be: i) reproduced or transmitted in any form, electronic or mechanical, including photocopying, recording or by means of any information storage or retrieval system without prior permission in writing from the publishers; or ii) used or reproduced in any way for the training, development or operation of artificial intelligence (AI) technologies, including generative AI technologies. The rights holders expressly reserve this publication from the text and data mining exception as per Article 4(3) of the Digital Single Market Directive (EU) 2019/790.

Bloomsbury Publishing Inc does not have any control over, or responsibility for, any third-party websites referred to or in this book. All internet addresses given in this book were correct at the time of going to press. The author and publisher regret any inconvenience caused if addresses have changed or sites have ceased to exist, but can accept no responsibility for any such changes.

A catalogue record for this book is available from the British Library.
Library of Congress Cataloging-in-Publication Data
Names: Goodland, Katharine, 1958- author.
Title: Shakespeare in the Theatre: Tina Packer / Katharine Goodland.
Description: London; New York: The Arden Shakespeare, 2024. |
Series: Shakespeare in the theatre; vol 15 | Includes bibliographical references and index.
Identifiers: LCCN 2023054086 (print) | LCCN 2023054087 (ebook) |
ISBN 9781350205710 (hardback) | ISBN 9781350205802 (paperback) |
ISBN 9781350205727 (ebook) | ISBN 9781350205734 (pdf)
Subjects: LCSH: Packer, Tina, 1938- | Shakespeare & Company (Lenox, Mass.) |
Shakespeare, William, 1564-1616–Stage history–Massachusetts–Lenox. |
Shakespeare, William, 1564-1616–Dramatic production. |
Theatrical producers and directors–United States–Biography.
Classification: LCC PN2287.P2 G66 2024 (print) | LCC PN2287.P2 (ebook) |
DDC 792.02/33092 [B]–dc23/eng/20240214
LC record available at https://lccn.loc.gov/2023054086
LC ebook record available at https://lccn.loc.gov/2023054087

ISBN: HB: 978-1-3502-0571-0
PB: 978-1-3502-0580-2
ePDF: 978-1-3502-0573-4
eBook: 978-1-3502-0572-7

Series: Shakespeare in the Theatre

Typeset by Deanta Global Publishing Services, Chennai, India

For product safety related questions contact productsafety@bloomsbury.com.

To find out more about our authors and books visit www.bloomsbury.com and sign up for our newsletters.

CONTENTS

List of Figures vi
Acknowledgements viii
Series Preface ix
Preface x

Introduction 1

1 For the joy of living in his great poetry 21

2 And we'll look, not at visions, but at realities 55

3 What a dream was here! 93

4 Kol Nidre 129

Appendix 169
Notes 178
References 186
Index 195

FIGURES

1. Outdoor mainstage at The Mount, 1980. Photo: Warren D. Fowler © F Scott Fowler. Reproduced courtesy of F. Scott Fowler 22
2. Ensemble: Oberon (Gregory Uel Cole), Fairy (Noni Pratt), Bottom (Jonathan Rutledge), Titania (Andrea Haring), Puck (Tony Simotes), Fairy (Susie Fugle), Fairy (Natsuko Ohama) and Fairy (Gina Weiss) in *A Midsummer Night's Dream*, mainstage at The Mount, 1978. Photo: Warren D. Fowler © F Scott Fowler. Reproduced courtesy of F. Scott Fowler 27
3. Ensemble: King of Naples (Herb Davis), Francisco (Brian Varga), Adrian (Garfield Randelman), Antonio (Kevin Coleman), Sebastian (David Breithbarth) and Gonzalo (Tom Kunis) in *The Tempest*, mainstage at The Mount, 1980, Photo: Warren D. Fowler © F Scott Fowler. Reproduced courtesy of F. Scott Fowler 38
4. Macbeth (Dan McCleary) and Spirits (L-R: Henry David Clarke, Judith McSpadden, Carolyn Roberts, Michael Hammond, Jennie Israel, Martin J. Asprey, Johnny Lee Davenport) in *Macbeth*, Founders' Theatre, 2002. Photo: Kevin Sprague © Kevin Sprague, 2002. Reproduced with the permission of Kevin Sprague 111
5. King John (Allyn Burrows) and Cardinal Pandulph (Mel Cobb) in *King John*, Founders' Theatre, 2005. Photo: Kevin Sprague © Kevin Sprague, 2002. Reproduced with the permission of Kevin Sprague 119
6. Arthur (Susannah Millonzi) and Hubert (Kenajuan Bentley) in *King John*, Founders' Theatre, 2005. Photo: Kevin Sprague © Kevin Sprague, 2002. Reproduced with the permission of Kevin Sprague 124

7   Nerissa (Annette Miller), Portia (Tod Randolph) and Prince of Morocco (John Douglas Thompson) with ensemble in *The Merchant of Venice*, mainstage at The Mount, 1998. Photo: Neil Hammer © Shakespeare & Company 1998. Reproduced with the permission of Stephen Ball, Shakespeare & Company 141

8   Guard (Thomas Brazzle), Antonio (John Hadden), Portia (Tamara Hickey) and Shylock (Jonathan Epstein) in *The Merchant of Venice*, The Tina Packer Playhouse, 2016. Photo: Ava G. Lindenmaier © Ava G. Lindenmaier 2016. Reproduced with the permission of Ava G. Lindenmaier 157

ACKNOWLEDGEMENTS

My utmost thanks go to Mark Dudgeon and his editorial team for the opportunity to publish this book as part of the *Shakespeare in the Theatre* series. Thanks especially to Stephen Purcell for his perceptive reading of the manuscript and Ella Wilson for her responsive guidance throughout the process. Giles Herman, Vishnu Prasad and their copy-editors were immensely helpful in the painstaking process of editing the manuscript. Thanks to my colleagues near and far who took time to speak with me: Steve Monte, Ken Gross, Lindsay Kaplan and Ayanna Thompson. Thank you to all the actors and creative artists who took time out of your hectic schedules to share memories of working with Tina Packer. Thanks to Melody Mason and Steve Ball for giving me access to the company archives. Thank you to my husband Don for being a thoughtful sounding board and a wonderful cook. Above all, thank you Tina Packer for your inspiring, visionary work.

SERIES PREFACE

Each volume in the *Shakespeare in the Theatre* series focuses on a director or theatre company who has made a significant contribution to Shakespeare production, identifying the artistic and political/social contexts of their work.

The series introduces readers to the work of significant theatre directors and companies whose Shakespeare productions have been transformative in our understanding of his plays in performance. Each volume examines a single figure or company, considering their key productions, rehearsal approaches and their work with other artists (actors, designers and composers). A particular feature of each book is its exploration of the contexts within which these theatre artists have made their Shakespeare productions work. Thus, the series not only considers the ways in which directors and companies produce Shakespeare but also reflects upon their other theatre activities and the broader artistic, cultural and sociopolitical milieu within which their Shakespeare performances and productions have been created. The key to the series' originality, then, is its consideration of Shakespeare production in a range of artistic and broader contexts; in this sense, it de-centres Shakespeare from within Shakespeare studies, pointing to the range of people, artistic practices and cultural phenomena that combine to make meaning in the theatre.

Series editors: Peter Holland, Farah Karim-Cooper and Stephen Purcell

PREFACE

The impetus for this book occurred a quarter of a century ago when Tina Packer responded to an email from a doctoral candidate whom she didn't know. It was March, 1999. I would never have guessed at the time that she was in the midst of the most difficult transition of her company's history. I was nearly done writing my dissertation on the representation of female mourning in early English drama, inspired by Richard Eyre's 1992 Royal National Theatre production of *Richard III* at Brooklyn Academy of Music. Ian McKellen's Richard garnered all the press, but what stayed with me were the scenes of the lamenting queens. A colleague who knew Packer encouraged me to write to her, explaining that Packer was deeply interested in women's mourning practices and their portrayal in Shakespeare. One afternoon I took a deep breath and sent a short message introducing myself, never expecting to hear from a busy artistic director of an important theatre company. That night around ten the phone rang. It was Tina Packer! We spoke for nearly an hour and she invited me to Harvard where she was directing *Richard III* for the Harvard-Radcliffe drama club.

Within a few hours of my visit, I was sighing out on sound up and down my spine, touching my toes and reaching for the sky alongside the student-actors led by the voice teacher, Kimberly White, who encouraged me to participate in the company's month-long training intensive. As a result of that workshop, I have first-hand knowledge of what it means for Shakespeare's language to become an actor's experience. Over the years I've participated in several workshops at Shakespeare & Company, from *First Folio* text with Dennis Krausnick to Clown with Michael Toomey, Dave Demke and Jane Nichols. I've also served as dramaturg on several productions.

Since 1999, I've seen many of the productions examined in this book. Throughout, my analysis of Packer's work draws on interviews with Tina Packer; the actors and designers who have worked with her; films and documents from the Shakespeare & Company archives; theatre reviews; and my first-hand experience of watching her direct. Tina Packer lives her vision. She wants everyone to achieve a deeper awareness of what is possible, finding and speaking truth with courage and openness, owning what we say, one word at a time.[1]

Introduction

'Here could I breathe my soul into the air'.
HENRY THE SIXTH, PART 2 (3.2.393)

On 2 July 2023 at 2.00 pm, Tina Packer's *Henry VI, Part 2: The Contention* began with a flourish of trumpets as the ten-member cast entered, positioning themselves beneath an enormous golden crown suspended from the heavens. I was seated two rows from the sparsely furnished stage: a prelate's pulpit loomed stage left and a king's throne sat expectantly beneath the pendent crown. The costumes evoked the play's late-medieval period while allowing for the actors' freedom of breath, body, voice and movement. On this summer Sunday afternoon, the Tina Packer Playhouse was full. The actors introduced themselves to the audience, naming the characters they played and with another flourish the play began. Packer's cast of ten playing multiple roles included Americans, British and Canadians, four of whom were Black and six of whom were white. They whirled around the stage and through the world of the play, deftly switching characters and genders while embodying Shakespeare's language in a polyphony of resonant voices and accents. What struck me about this mingling is not that it is unique with respect to how Shakespeare is performed in America today, but rather that it is continuous with the work Tina Packer has produced for nearly half a century.

When Packer founded Shakespeare & Company in Lenox, Massachusetts in 1978, colourblind casting held sway in Shakespearean performance across the country while actors on both sides of the Atlantic were often trained to standardize their native accents. Packer never subscribed to either of these practices. She sees theatre as the space for discovering and revealing ourselves rather than trying to change or hide who we are while pretending that we can or should be blind to others. In the autumn of 1978, shortly after the company's inaugural performance, Packer hosted a weekend symposium in conjunction with the Black National Theatre of Harlem and the Freedom Theatre of Philadelphia to explore the question, 'What is Classical Theatre?' Twenty people stayed for the weekend, sharing ideas about the nature and purpose of classical theatre in American society. They reached a consensus that articulated an aspiration: 'Classical theatre embodies the highest truths, universally told, that have healing power' (Packer 2020b). This is not an expression of Shakespeare's oeuvre as *a priori* universal. Rather, it means that when performed with a multicultural cast embodying the story ('universally told'), classical plays possess the potential for healing, of individuals as well as society. Packer explained, 'It seemed to us self-evident that you had to have multicultural cast, because we live in a multicultural world and even if not all the races and cultures get on with each other, we must engage in the action of finding each other's humanity and the deepest things about us that connect us' (2020b). Packer recalled that the company's 1979 production of *Romeo and Juliet* exemplified this potential:

> Juliet, Natsuko Ohama, was Japanese Canadian, Capulet was Joe Marcell, a West Indian Englishman, and Lady Capulet was a white American. Now, when the audience first sees the Capulet family, they might be distracted in some way … But once the actors reach them through the language – as they engage with each other as husband, wife, child, mother, father – the story takes over … The verbal always has to lead the visual … You keep on working towards the kind of society that you believe in. (2020b)

What Packer means by the verbal leading the visual is not that the production is colourblind but instead the opposite. When the actors inhabit the language as their experience, the depth of the performance resonates with the audience so that whatever initial resistance they feel falls away as they realize that what they see is indeed a family. As Amy Cook puts it, 'Casting is how we rehearse change, as we come to see an expanded repertoire of the kinds of bodies that are selected to play the lead, the hero, and the villain' (Cook 2020: iii). On the other hand, she points out, 'casting is never politically or ideologically neutral' (Cook 2020: 2). Moreover, Ania Loomba notes that 'casting cannot by itself change the meaning of "color" or identity on the stage' (2006: xvi). Packer's approach to multicultural Shakespeare, developed in collaboration with two venerable Black theatre companies, began nearly three decades before Shakespearean theatre in America had the benefit of these insights. Even so, Packer never thought of casting or Shakespeare's language as in and of themselves agents of change. Rather, the dynamic creative engagement of actors with Shakespeare's language results in performances with the potential to shift our understanding of ourselves and each other. Packer's original method, *dropping in*, is premised upon the actors having creative agency in developing their characters.[1] Her process encourages the actors to engage with their characters through a deep symbiotic process. The actors do not simply take on the characteristics of the role they play: their identities and emotions also deeply inform their characters.[2]

Packer places the actors' creativity at the centre of her process and their engagement with Shakespeare's language at the centre of their performances. For her, 'the creative energy of the actors is what make plays work' (2020c). 'Creative', in Packer's formulation, refers to each actor's artistic agency in the process of making theatre: bringing their character into being, forming relationships with the other characters, moving through the space and engaging with the audience. 'Energy' refers to 'the performer's nervous and muscular power', which 'exists … in any living body' (Taviani 2005: 72). For performance, this 'nervous and muscular power' requires conscious shaping to enable actors, 'to act, to move, to be present, in an effective theatrical way' (2005: 72). Theatrical traditions around the world, from Kabuki to Stella Adler, have developed techniques for shaping this energy into what is referred to as the actor's 'presence', meaning that the actor's energy has been shaped in a theatrically effective way.[3] As Eugenio Barba explains:

> A body-in-life is more than a body merely alive. A body-in-life dilates the performer's presence and the spectator's perception ... The flow of energies that characterise our daily behaviour has been re-routed. The tensions that secretly govern our normal way of being physically present come to the surface in the performer, become visible, unexpectedly ... The dilated body is above all a glowing body, in the scientific sense of the term: the particles that make up daily behaviour have been excited and produce more energy, they have undergone an increment of motion, they move further apart, attract and oppose each other with more force, in a restricted or expanded space. (Barba 2005: 52–3)

The moulding of the actors' energy 'according to non-daily modalities' (Taviani 2005: 72) is fundamental to the artistic process, both collectively, from the director's perspective, as well as individually, as each actor discovers how their character speaks, moves and interacts with the other characters and the audience. Packer's process focusses on releasing, encouraging, observing and guiding this energy in every area of production, from working with her cast on Shakespeare's language to shaping the production's design, music and sound. As Packer writes, 'Shakespeare wrote plays that demand an active participation of all people involved; the way he wrote has as a prerequisite the creativity of others. Without the truth of others, the plays do not exist. And every single production is a unique collaborative act ... This collaborative play is the energy that forms the world the characters live in' (Packer 2016: xii).

How does the energy of 'collaborative play' shape the world of the characters? Packer establishes an environment where 'collaborative play' is itself the process that she guides in eight phases, each based upon inquiry. The actors' individual nervous and muscular power collide during the collaborative play of rehearsal, building the world of the performance, a world comprised of their energy that continuously regenerates and reshapes their individual energies and the energy of the world of the play. In the most basic sense this phenomenon happens constantly as we move through our daily lives. Each person's nervous and muscular power is in constant flux, changing according to the surroundings and interactions with others. It is also what happens when a director plans the staging in advance. As the actors follow a director's staging, their energy will change and that will change how they relate to each other, thereby altering the energy of the play's world. Packer works in a different direction, stimulating her actors' creative energy and then shaping the production based upon what she sees happening with the energies of the specific cast she is directing at the time:

> I like the actors to find their characters and relationships through *dropping in* and the flow of their scene, through rehearsal.[4] At that point I'll start working with what they are doing because I can see from the outside what's happening, shifting and altering what they've given me to make it align with everything else in the play. And they own it – they are not trying to do what I've told them to do ... This is political for me in as much as one of the most important functions of art is to encourage people to think afresh. I want the actors to be in touch with their own creativity rather than do something because they are following my direction. (2021a)

Shaping the Actors' Energy

Each step of Packer's process is designed to generate and guide the actors' creative energy, so that when they are on stage in front of an audience they are not bodies merely alive, they are bodies-in-life. What follows is a summary of Packer's process of guiding her actors from page to stage.[5]

1. Focussing the cast. Packer reaches out by email to cast members a week or so before the first rehearsal, usually with a question to focus them on some aspect of the play they will be working on. She might ask them to write a journal entry about their identity, the nature of violence, an important memory or a line of poetry or phrase that is meaningful to them.[6]

2. Checking in. Each day of rehearsal begins with a thirty minute 'check-in' with the entire cast. The check-ins are an integral part of the 'collective telling of the story of the play' (Packer 2020c). Whenever the cast meets, they sit in chairs in a circle, so that their bodies, hearts, minds and energies (nervous and muscular power) are open to each other. The circle is the safe space for sharing insights about the play based upon what arises in rehearsal. If it is the first day of rehearsal, Packer may ask them to share their response to her pre-rehearsal prompt. Someone will speak first on impulse. When finished, that person turns to look at the person next to them indicating it is their turn. It doesn't matter whether it is to the right or the left. The check-in then proceeds in that direction. Each person speaks in turn without crosstalk or discussion until everyone has spoken. The ritual forecloses a hierarchical structure of raising hands and being called on by the director. It promotes deep listening while developing relationships and impulses among the cast that carry over into performance. Often Packer includes check-ins at the end of the day when the rehearsal process is especially intense, or if there was a significant discovery that needs to be shared. Over time these check-ins take on the character of connective tissue among the cast as the ritual of sharing insights and discoveries draws the cast together and feeds their creative energy.

3. *Dropping in* is, in many ways, the heart of Packer's process.

Scene partners sit across from one another in chairs with their backs long, maintaining eye contact, breathing deeply, remaining open and relaxed, sitting closely enough for their knees to slightly overlap, with hands resting gently on their thighs. Each actor has a director or associate director sitting slightly behind and to the side of them with the script, to drop in each word or phrase, prompting the actor to respond imaginatively to questions that they ask in a neutral tone. For example, 'Love. What does love, mean to you? Love'. The actor repeats the word as they breathe out, exploring the feelings and thoughts that emerge while maintaining eye contact with their scene partner, continuing to breathe deeply. The actors do not share their thoughts aloud; rather, what they are feeling will be carried on the contours of their voice as they repeat the word. The director and assistant directors help to keep the actors focussed and relaxed. Breaks are usually needed about every twenty minutes and are also taken as necessary.

The sessions are by design intense, emotional, and ultimately, exhilarating. The language and the feelings and thoughts become one. Packer's method elicits the creativity of the actors as they freely associate with key words of their text while speaking the words to their scene partner. The process connects them with the immense range of their own creativity as they surprise themselves with connections and meanings, both conscious and unconscious, while realizing how rapidly they can move through many emotions and shades of feeling, a necessary skill in the performance of Shakespeare's plays. His characters shift rapidly through intense emotions, even in a single line of iambic pentameter. Packer and her vocal experts teach that each breath is an inspiration, each breath is an opportunity to begin again, opening up the possibility for discovery and connection, connection with the words, the psyche and between scene partners. The lifeblood of a production is created breath by breath, word by word, resonating through, between and among the actors in a production. The process of *dropping in* the text of the play liberates and develops this creative energy. It is a demanding artistic process that requires concentration and openness, focus as well as permeability, stillness as well as a willingness to explore, and the flexibility to make discoveries and just as easily let each discovery go with the next breath. The goal for each actor is artistic realization, encouraging them to forge a deep, unique connection with their character's language and their scene partners.

As Packer explains, the process of *dropping in* allows 'meaning to come through the language' as it moves through the actor, 'as opposed to actors using the language to reflect their inner mutterings. They're very different ways of acting' (2020c). *Dropping in* invites the actors to inhabit the language as their experience in a symbiotic relationship with their personal memories and imagination. The acting occurs through the speaking of the words; the words themselves convey the character's thoughts and emotions. This may seem rather obvious, yet I have seen plenty of actors who report the emotion on top of or between the words instead of inhabiting and experiencing them. For example, in Shakespeare's *Troilus and Cressida*, Act 3, scene 2, Troilus is 'giddy' and 'whirled around' by 'expectation' as he awaits his first meeting with Cressida. The specific feeling of expectation expressed in this moment has a forceful physical dimension that requires embodiment. When the actor inhabits the emotion, the vibrations can reach the audience through the actor's voice. The process encourages the actors to open their psyches as well as their physical awareness, tapping into their unique creativity, opening their voices to the power of their breath. Their characters' identities emerge from this unique encounter between actor and text. Through *dropping in* actors discover their own answers to their characters' natures and dilemmas. Their language is clear and resonant because they have made the words of Shakespeare's text their own, creating a shared history with their scene partners and a personal history with Shakespeare's words. Through the demanding and exhilarating process of *dropping in*, Shakespeare's words merge with the actor's psyche in a dynamic artistic encounter as the actor actively creates and discovers their character through an embodied visceral experience with the language of the text.

Packer devised *dropping in* specifically for directing Shakespeare's plays. As with any technique of shaping actors' energy into non-daily modalities, there are those who prefer other methods. Some prefer table work, others feel they can discover the specificity necessary for effectively speaking the language through practice, a good dictionary and a director who helps them find that specificity or tells them what to do. Many actors who have worked with Packer, however, find *dropping in* to be effective and efficient because they are encouraged to draw on deeply held memories and the 'DNA of the word', as Packer puts it (2023b). Through this method 'they discover things they didn't know they knew before they began the process' (2023b). Following are three representative testimonies from actors who have been directed by Packer.

Deaon Griffin-Pressley, who, upon graduating from high school, won an award to study Shakespeare at the British-American Academy at Oxford University, related that *dropping in* during the rehearsal process 'allowed me to drop into my authenticity and voice a lot more organically, without judgment; it allowed me to open up to Shakespeare in a way that I had not been able to do before in terms of how I perceive myself as an African American, and as a man'(2021). Cloteal L. Horne recalled that 'To go through the rigor of *dropping in* that full text was really deep. I was dreaming more than I usually do. My subconscious was waking up in really fruitful ways that was fueling my understanding of Salarino' (2022). Peter Macon appreciated how *dropping in* taught him a way of 'getting the words in your molecules ... I am glad I was able to do the work with Shakespeare & Company because it set a precedent for how I have approached Shakespeare since then' (2022). He admired the 'intensive level of practice' at the company, recalling that Packer gave everyone a sense of mission in what they were doing: 'We're not up here performing for entertainment. We are up here baring ourselves and being the conduit of all our collective consciousness ... We wanted to speak to the audience on that visceral level' (2022).

4. Staging scenes. Packer stages the play after *dropping in* because she wants the actors to build the emotional world of the play as the foundation for building the world of the production. During this step Packer introduces the themes and form of the play that are pertinent to this particular cast. At this stage the cast rotates through scene work (broken down into beats), through

vocal work, movement, dance, fight and text. Each of these areas is led by the company's master trainers while the scene rehearsals are led by Packer, along with two or three associate directors, so that the scene rehearsals can be scheduled simultaneously. Packer's use of associate directors has helped to train and develop many who are now directors in their own right.

5. The stumble through. Following scene rehearsal Packer guides the cast in a 'stumble through' of the entire play. The actors are expected to be more or less off book and to perform according to how their scenes were staged during scene rehearsal. Assistants are on hand with scripts to 'feed in' (cue) the lines as needed. During the 'stumble through' Packer carefully observes what is happening in the dynamic between the world of the play and the world of the production and makes necessary adjustments. As I note in Chapter 4, when rehearsal time was cut in half, Packer adapted her method by changing the 'stumble through' after scene rehearsal to a 'stagger through' on the first day. The 'stagger through' invites the actors to be uninhibited. It frees them to focus on their personal engagement with the role, without judgment. The name of the exercise includes a pun, as Packer explains: 'It brings out staggering insights because the actors support each other and feed off of each other's energy' (2023b). I discuss this further in Chapter 4.

6. Group movement exercises. Packer uses large-scale exercises with the entire cast or groups of actors as necessary. These exercises encourage the cast to embody key elements of the play. For example, rather than discussing social status or religious identity during Shakespeare's time, she uses exercises such as the 'Power Walk' and 'Who is a Jew?' (discussed in Chapter 4), to help them viscerally experience the emotional dimensions of class, racial prejudice and anti-Semitism. Her exercises are inspired by the plays themselves, as I discuss in detail in Chapters 2 and 4.

7. Entering the space. Following the 'stumble through', the cast does as many 'run-throughs' of the play in the performance space as needed and time permits in order to confirm the staging and make final adjustments.

8. The Technical rehearsal. This final step before the first dress rehearsal ensures that the cast understands the sound, music and lighting cues.[7]

By the end of the rehearsal period, the actors have created their characters from the inside out. The words of the text have become their experience, an experience of inhabiting the language that is then shared with the audience. In this state of being, the actors embody the capacity to 'produce an effect' in themselves as well as others (*Oxford English Dictionary*, *s. v.* 'Energy').

Philosophically, Packer's emphasis on the energy of the actors as the centre of the theatrical experience aligns with Hannah Arendt's discussion of 'Aristotle's notion of *energeia* ("actuality")' (206), as a 'specifically human achievement' (207). *Energeia*, one of the etymological roots for 'energy', defines, as Arendt explains, 'all activities that do not pursue an end (are *ateleis*) and leave no work behind (no par autas erga), but exhaust their full meaning in the performance itself ... The performance is the work, is energeia' (206). The energy of this work emerges through the actors' symbiotic creative encounter with Shakespeare's language, word by word. Moreover, as Arendt explains, it is through language that human beings 'make [their] appearance in the human world' (Arendt 1998: 179). If we replace 'make' and 'appearance' here with their synonyms, 'create' and 'identity', Arendt's observation illuminates the actors' art. For it is in the public space of the theatre where actors explore, by means of language, the complex dimensions of human identity and experience.

Shaping the company: Beginnings to the present

Packer's emphasis on the importance of the actor's creative role in the process grew out of her own experience as an actor. Having graduated from the Royal Academy of Dramatic Art (RADA) in 1964 with Honours, Packer embarked on a successful acting career. In nearly every instance, however, she wanted the progression from page to performance to draw more deeply on the actors' creative impulses. She decided to chart her own course and learn to a direct as a means to understand, 'how to create theatre that honors its transformative potential' (Merlin and Packer 2020: 11).[8] With this question as her lodestar, she 'parlayed [her] acting credentials into a position as a director at LAMDA (London Academy of Music and Drama)' (2020a), where, in 1971, she was hired to direct twelve productions over the next two years, six of them by Shakespeare. Her experience at LAMDA shaped the ethos and organization of Shakespeare & Company, which from the beginning has had influential training and education components. The voice training in particular appealed to Packer's desire for visceral depth in the creative process. The vocal work was built on the legacy of Iris Warren whose technique focussed on releasing 'the physical and mental tensions caused by blocked emotions' rather than emphasizing 'the voice beautiful' (Linklater 2006: 6). Above all, it led Packer to Kristin Linklater, whose method of freeing the actors' natural voices was instrumental to Packer's vision and approach to directing: 'Meeting Kristin was a huge step forward … Her work was based on the deep connection between body, breath, and sound, and how connected sound opened up creative impulses and affected the psyche' (Packer 2020a). Linklater, who was Scottish, was a voice expert and vocal coach who had taken up Warren's mantle at LAMDA before moving to the States in 1963 to train actors across the country while developing her original voice progression. When Packer learned from one of her American students with a contact at the Ford Foundation that the organization was supporting theatre research, she set off for the States with two goals: to meet Kristin Linklater and to pursue Ford Foundation funding for research into another question that occurred to her while she was directing Shakespeare at LAMDA: 'What is it that makes Shakespearean Theatre so vibrant and lasting that it is still performed to this day?' (2020a).

Packer and Linklater quickly recognized that their ideas for creating theatre dovetailed. Both had worked with American and British actors and agreed that a fusion of their respective strengths was worth exploring as a way to develop a visceral approach to contemporary Shakespearean theatre. As a generalization, they felt that Americans were more willing to probe their psyches while British actors were more skilled in technique. Meanwhile, Richard Kapp, the programming officer at the Ford Foundation, found Packer's passion, eloquence and ideas for a British-American company persuasive. Even though Packer herself was British, her idea for developing Shakespeare actor training for Americans was highly appealing at a time when the foundation was supporting regional theatre in America, and there was a dearth of skilled artists to train actors in the structure of the verse, voice, movement, fight and dance. Packer was awarded funding to support a ten-month practice-based experiment that brought together British and American master teachers with fifteen American, Canadian, South African and British actors to train for performance in five key areas identified as essential for Elizabethan theatre: '(1) structure of the verse; (2) voice and language; (3) fight; (4) movement; and (5) the actor/audience relationship' (Merlin and Packer 2020: 18).[9] The project took place from February to November 1973, beginning in Alcester, England (near Stratford-upon-Avon), with four months of intensive training, and concluding in America with the project's culminating performances of *The Taming of the Shrew* at the O'Neill Centre and the Performing Garage. Packer drew on the connections she made as an actor, gathering master teachers who were among the most renowned in the world: John Barton (structure of the verse), B. H. Barry (fight) and John Broome (dance). Kristin Linklater, the voice master teacher for the experiment, brought in Trish Arnold (movement). The artists welcomed the opportunity to come together for an intensive period of time to share their ideas and participate in each other's workshops. In the early years after Packer founded her company, Kristin Linklater, B. H. Barry and John Broome worked on her productions and began to train the actors interested in teaching: Tony Simotes, Kevin Coleman, Gregory Uel Cole and Corinna May (fight); Susan Dibble (dance and movement). These younger artists then carried the work forward. Dennis Krausnick took up text and voice work, inspired by John Barton, Packer's mentor at the RSC, who became a close friend and visited Shakespeare & Company over the years.

The Ford-funded experiment, Packer's 'first company' (2020a), laid the groundwork for Shakespeare & Company's unique approach to training and performance, built on these five elements. The sixth, clown, was added when Merry Conway joined the company as clownmaster in 1981. Packer's production of *The Taming of the Shrew*, the culminating product of the experiment, impressed McNeil Lowry, head of the Arts and Humanities Division at the Ford Foundation (Merlin and Packer 2020: 25). He championed Packer for a travel and study grant to learn about 'other world views and cultures', in order to enlarge her understanding of classical theatre (Merlin and Packer 2020: 25–6). Packer spent nearly eighteen months travelling, from 1974 to 1976, exploring the relationship between Sanskrit and music in India, the political theatre of Brazil, movement with Moshé Feldenkrais in Israel, *Commedia dell'arte* and clowning in Italy and Peter Brook's multi-ethnic, international company in France (Packer 2020a). As Packer neared the end of her travels, she received an invitation from Kristin Linklater, who was on the theatre faculty at New York University (NYU), to direct a Shakespeare play for the theatre programme that explored violence. It was there in 1976 that she met several actors who would join her company in less than two years, one of whom was Dennis Krausnick, a Jesuit priest turned actor, who with Kristin Linklater, co-founded the company with Packer.[10] Kevin Coleman, head of the company's education programme, joined them in 1979. After directing at NYU, Packer returned to England to lead Shakespeare workshops and direct in London. She then returned to the States in the autumn of 1977, having been invited to direct Moliere's *Learned Ladies* for the theatre programme at Smith

College. The production was included among a total of eight college productions selected from across the country to perform at the Kennedy Center in Washington, D.C.[11] This programme continues today, honouring outstanding college productions with the opportunity to perform for a general audience at one of the country's premier theatres.

Early in 1978, while preparing her cast for the Kennedy Center performance, Packer set to work on a plan to establish a classical theatre company in one of the vacant spaces available on Forty-Second street in New York City.[12] As she pondered all that she had learnt over the past seven years, she penned a letter of thanks to Richard Kapp, elucidating her findings. At the heart of her discoveries was her conviction that theatre's transformative potential is realized through the shared experience of language between actor and audience. Moreover, theatre 'becomes electric' she wrote, when the actors inhabit Shakespeare's words 'as a musical instrument is its notes' (Packer letter to Kapp, 1 March 1978; cited in Merlin and Packer 2020: 33). When Kapp received her letter, he invited to her to visit his home in Chappaqua, New York, introducing her to Mitch Berenson, a former Longshoreman turned real estate developer. Berenson, taken by Packer's intelligence, confidence and the clarity and size of her ambition, suggested she consider forming her company in the Berkshires. The area had Tanglewood, the Williamstown Theatre Festival, and Jacob's Pillow among other cultural attractions. During the summer months Bostonians and New Yorkers, as well as others from farther away, flocked to the area, seeking culture away from the city heat among the rolling hills of Berkshire County. What the Berkshires didn't have was a Shakespeare theatre. Berenson, who was interested in seeing Packer direct, offered to drop in on her rehearsal at Smith College in Northampton the next weekend to watch her rehearsal and then drive her around the area to show her the available properties. That Saturday in the cold April twilight, they drove to Edith Wharton's abandoned estate on the outskirts of Lenox, Massachusetts. When Packer saw The

Mount, built by Wharton in 1902 on plans inspired by Belton House, a seventeenth-century Grade 1 listed English country house, she looked, not with her eyes but with her mind. She saw beyond the boarded-up windows and ice-covered floors to what it would become.

Packer has never explained what it was that drew her to The Mount. At the time it required hundreds of thousands of dollars of repair. Founding a Shakespeare company was challenge enough, yet she took on the daunting task of restoring the 16,850 square foot main house at the same time that she was building her company. The property sits on 49.5 acres and includes Wharton's Stable and Garden House, also in need of work, along with overgrown lawns and gardens. Packer's company members say that she knows magic when she sees it. The Mount is indeed a magic place, with its elaborate Italianate terrace and lawns sloping down to gardens and stands of stately spruce trees bordered by Laurel Lake. Yet, I can't help but think that what bewitched Packer that evening emanated from her English roots. In our first interview Packer explained that, 'it was Shakespeare's own world that was drawing' her to want to have her own company (2020a). Here in the Berkshires of America was an echo of that world of Arden. Packer knew well the Elizabethan tradition of touring companies that performed at country estates for the nobility throughout England. Here, with her 'risen working class roots' (Merlin and Packer 2020: 10), Packer would transform that tradition. Her multicultural company would perform, not for nobility, but for audiences of all ages and social standing, and they would do so in their native accents with their natural voices. And it would all happen here, on an estate built by a woman who was a writer, as Packer had once thought she might be. Here could she breathe her soul into the air.

At the time Edith Wharton's life and work were gradually being recovered. In 1975 Harper and Row published F. R. Leavis's biography of Wharton while feminist academics were steadily restoring women writers to their rightful place in the American literary canon. Packer and her company played a significant role in the renewal of interest in Edith Wharton and her estate: so much so, that in two decades time, they would lose it. Soon after Shakespeare & Company occupied The Mount, Packer realized she needed a different plan for managing the company while restoring The Mount. Dennis Krausnick and Mitch Berenson helped her form a second not-for-profit: Edith Wharton Restoration, Inc., which purchased the property in 1980 to restore the estate as well as ensure that if Shakespeare & Company 'went bust' as Packer put it, 'the house and grounds would not go down as well' (2020a). The arrangement was intended to be mutually beneficial. Shakespeare & Company was the only tenant, paying rent that helped to fund the restoration. Several members of the company initially served on the board of Edith Wharton Restoration, Inc. Over time the composition of the board changed, with fewer representatives of Shakespeare & Company. As restoration of the estate proceeded apace so did Shakespeare & Company's success and acclaim, drawing increasing audiences to the estate as well as those who were primarily interested in Edith Wharton and wanted to tour the house. Shakespeare & Company promoted Edith Wharton's novels and stories. They used her original Salon in the house for readings and performances. Dennis Krausnick adapted many of Wharton's short stories into one-act plays that were performed by the company. In the wake of Martin Scorsese's 1993 film *The Age of Innocence*, interest grew exponentially. Over the next few years, Wharton Restoration, Inc. began the process of evicting the company, accusing the troupe of damaging the rooms and grounds and not being responsive to requests for tours.[13]

A lengthy arbitration process ensued and, in 2001, Shakespeare & Company left The Mount, having found a new home in the heart of Lenox on Kemble Street.[14] This sixty-three-acre property, initially three separate estates that were joined to create a boy's school, had outbuildings and meadows that in the right light evoked an Elizabethan village. Thanks to a ten-million-dollar campaign led by board Chair Mike Miller and Tina Packer, the company had a new theatre ready to welcome audiences the same summer they were saying farewell to The Mount. Designed by British theatre consultant

Iain Mackintosh and American architect George E. Marsh, Jr., it was retrofitted into the former school's gymnasium with such skill that no trace of its former existence remains. The new space, dubbed, 'Founders' Theatre', since renamed 'The Tina Packer Playhouse', seats over four-hundred, configured with a deep thrust stage or in the round on two levels that keep the audience close to the action.

Galvanized by the possibilities of the company's new home, Packer set to work on an ambitious project to build a replica of The Rose Theatre. A clever fund-raising campaign invited donors to 'buy a stake in The Rose'. The names of donors were painted on wooden stakes used to establish the footprint of the theatre. A stake bearing Judi Dench's name, among many others, remains in what is now The Rose Footprint theatre. The early years of the twenty-first century saw 9/11 and the financial collapse of 2008, causing the company to scale down its financial obligations. The Rose Footprint theatre lives on in hope as a 'reconstruction of the first level of Shakespeare's first London theatre', hosting productions under its tented roof for up to 250.[15]

If the Kemble Street property does not have the English country house ambiance of The Mount, what it does have are all the necessary spaces for a year-round theatre company that conducts training and education as well as performances. The Miller Building houses the administration offices and archives. Larry Hall is a dormitory for those participating in productions and training. The Elayne Bernstein building has three state-of-the-art rehearsal studios, a set shop, and an indoor theatre. The Roman Garden Theatre is a 280-seat open-air space, and the Arthur S. Waldstein Amphitheater is an open-air amphitheatre that seats 540. Backed by a stand of towering spruce trees and surrounded by the audience on three sides, it reimagines the company's former outdoor mainstage at The Mount.[16]

As with the company's location and venues, its organization has changed while retaining the imprint of the early years. The company's three branches – performance, training and education – have existed from the beginning. Now entering its forty-sixth year, Shakespeare & Company has twenty-six full-time year-round employees, twelve of whom are theatre artists who are also managers, including Allyn Burrows, the company's artistic director.[17] In the late spring and summer months this number swells to over one hundred, while increasing again slightly for the annual Fall Festival of high school productions in October and November. Over the decades, Shakespeare & Company has developed an extended member network of working artists all over the country, many of whom have positions in theatre companies, some who have founded their own companies, and others who are tenured faculty in university theatre departments. Many return regularly to lead workshops and perform in or direct productions. For example. Kenneth Ransom, a member of the company in the early decades, returned in the summer of 2023 to play Somerset and Hume in Packer's production of *The Contention*. He is now a professor of theatre at Emerson college.

The company's abiding commitment to creating immediate theatre was evident in every aspect of Packer's 2023 production of *The Contention*. The vibrations of the actors' voices resounded through the intimate space. The audience was visible to everyone in the theatre, while the actors emerged from every corner and level, drawing us in, implicating us in the production's excavation of violence and thirst for power.

This book

This book gives a comprehensive account of Tina Packer's Shakespearean body of work from the founding of the company in 1978 to the present, examining her productions chronologically by decade in four chapters that trace the development of her three different styles: (1) Her grand mise en scène productions, developed for the expansive outdoor mainstage at The Mount, where she deployed casts of forty or more;[18] (2) Her bare bard style, originated for the 180 seat indoor Stables theatre at The Mount, with casts of six to eight actors playing all the roles; (3) Her playhouse style, developed for the indoor theatre that bears her name, using cast sizes between eight and eighteen. Each chapter is framed by a narrative survey of her directing and acting careers. Within this running narrative, I explore in more depth selected productions that demonstrate how her collaborative approach to directing resulted in productions that astonished audiences with the clarity of the language and resonance of the storytelling. Chapter 1 surveys the plays of her first decade, exploring in greater depth how Packer used the features of the open-air setting at The Mount to immerse the audience in the worlds of *A Midsummer Night's Dream*, *The Tempest* and *Twelfth Night*. Chapter 2 surveys the plays of her second decade, beginning with a close up of how Packer worked with three different actors on her 1988 *As You Like It* for the outdoor mainstage. At the centre of the chapter, we move indoors for a look at two productions of her acclaimed bare bard style, *Julius Caesar* and *Measure for Measure*, developed for the indoor Stables theatre at The Mount. Chapter 3 focuses on the plays of her third decade when her productions became more overtly political. I explore how Packer's 2001 *Midsummer Night's Dream* helped her company and audience work through the loss of The Mount. Subsequently, her 2002 *Macbeth* and 2005 *King John* engaged in searching critiques of warfare over time, including the first decade of the twenty-first century in America. Chapter 4 surveys the productions of her fourth decade, when she stepped aside as artistic director, taking on an advisory role in the company under her new title, 'Founding Artistic Director'. At the centre of this final chapter, I examine the two productions of *The Merchant of Venice* that Packer directed nearly two decades apart in very different spaces and rehearsal conditions. The first was produced in 1998 for the expansive open-air mainstage at The Mount with eight weeks of rehearsal. The second was performed indoors in 2016 in the intimate space of the Tina Packer Playhouse with only four weeks allotted for rehearsal. My analysis of these two productions demonstrates the effectiveness and adaptability of Packer's approach under different circumstances. I conclude this exploration of her work showing how in 2016 her approach to directing produced an original, timely interpretation of *The Merchant of Venice* with a multicultural cast.[19]

1

For the joy of living in his great poetry[1]

In its first decade Shakespeare & Company grew into one of the most significant regional companies in the northeast, staging seventeen Shakespeare productions and fifteen new play adaptations of Edith Wharton's short stories. The company's work was regularly reviewed in *The New York Times*, *Christian Science Monitor*, *The Boston Globe*, *Shakespeare Quarterly*, *Shakespeare Bulletin*, and several prominent New England newspapers. As artistic director, Packer oversaw the increase of the company's summer programming from two productions in 1978 to eight by 1987. In the midst of a completely full calendar, Packer accepted an invitation to step up as artistic director of the Boston Shakespeare Company in 1984 when Peter Sellars left for the Kennedy Center. Packer saw this as an opportunity to have a year-round performance space in Boston's cultural district. During the final three years of the decade, she worked tirelessly with a commercial investor on a project to build a theatre and rehearsal studio in a commercial building one block from Boston's Symphony Hall. The plan was foiled by an economic downturn (King 1989: 31). Early in her second decade, Packer, ever resourceful in the face of obstacles, opened an indoor space in Edith Wharton's former stable at The Mount.

FIGURE 1 *Outdoor mainstage at The Mount, 1980. Photo: Warren D. Fowler © F Scott Fowler. Reproduced courtesy of F. Scott Fowler.*

This chapter surveys the twelve Shakespeare productions Packer directed during her first decade, including in-depth explorations of *A Midsummer Night's Dream* (1978), the company's inaugural play; *The Tempest* (1980), starring Harris Yulin and Joe Morton; and *Twelfth Night* (1981 and 1982), featured in Joseph Papp's *Celebrate Brooklyn* series. This chapter focuses in particular on two significant and original aspects of her work: her virtuosic use of the open-air natural amphitheatre and her multicultural approach to Shakespeare (Figure 1).

Merging worlds: *A Midsummer Night's Dream*, 1978

On 21 July 1978, Shakespeare & Company's *A Midsummer Night's Dream* opened to 'several hundred spectators' in the natural amphitheatre at The Mount (Merlin and Packer 2020: 40). The play was an astute choice. It is perhaps Shakespeare's most beloved and well-known play while being well-suited for outdoor theatre in midsummer. It introduced the community to Tina Packer's signature style: the audience–actor relationship was foremost in Packer's imaginative, site-specific use of the space and the play's story was told with energy, depth and clarity. Each actor's natural, unamplified voice resonated with the audience in the evening air: 'Tina Packer directed her company to present Shakespeare classically, for the people – nothing high and mighty about it, down to earth and with a strong emphasis on the word' (Salsbury 1979: 178). Packer transported her audience into the world of her *Dream* by using the qualities of the estate to immerse them in the action between Athens and the wood.

The audience sat on blankets on the estate's wide grassy slope leading down from the main house to a flat, open area carpeted with pine needles that was backed by a stand of towering spruce trees. Here, the fairy court held sway. Behind and above the natural amphitheatre where the audience sat was a spacious Italianate terrace on the mansion's east façade that served as Theseus's palace. The performance began when Theseus (Dennis Krausnick), donning a long red robe, and Hippolyta (Gillian Barge), draped in purple, appeared on the terrace, inviting the audience to turn around and look up, a physical movement that placed them as subjects to these ancient royal figures as Hippolyta 'raised her arms to the sky' (Salsbury 1978: 177). In response to Theseus's impatience for their nuptial hour, Barge's Hippolyta invoked the play's prologue and theme with her resonant voice, further drawing them into the play's world: 'Four days will quickly steep themselves in night / Four night's will quickly dream away the time; / And then the moon, like to a silver bow, / New bent in heaven, Shall behold the night / Of our solemnities' (1.1.7–11). When the lovers fled to the wood, the audience was surrounded. Actors entered the flat open playing area below from all sides: behind the audience, down the slope, through the woods. At times they seemed to fly, sweeping in on ropes hung from the trees (Salsbury 1979: 177).

The fairies, an integral part of the setting, were wild earthy creatures, scantily clad in short, ragged skirts and 'leather bodices with acorns or sprigs of pine in their hair' (Haring 2022). Andrea Haring, who played Titania, explained that during the rehearsal process the actors cast as fairies explored their world through improvisations that clarified what 'it meant to be elemental and the fact that we've existed since the earth began. We were forever young and yet old in spirit' (2022). Through *dropping in* Haring found Titania's empathy for the mother of the 'changeling boy' (2.1.120): 'My connection with my attendant deeply moved me to understand what it meant for the Queen of the fairies to have a friendship with a mortal woman. My promise to her that I would rear her child when she died was a solemn oath to me, and I had to honour it' (2022). Packer's *dropping in*, as explained in the introduction, draws on the actors' creativity through the process of asking questions, word by word, sequentially through the text, in order to forge an experiential, creative connection between the words and images of the text with the actor's imagination. Titania articulates in detailed imagery the intimacy shared between the queen of the fairies and her votress:

> she gossiped by my side / And sat with me on Neptune's yellow sands ... we have laughed to see the sails conceive / and grow big bellied with the wanton wind; / Which she, with pretty and with swimming gait, / Following, her womb then rich with my young squire, / Would imitate and sail upon the land / To fetch me trifles. (2.1.125–133)

Certainly, an actor can understand the depth of this relationship as expressed in the verse. *Dropping in* can create a deeper experience of the words because the process requires the actor's creative and imaginative engagement with each word: Haring experienced the friendship word by word through *dropping in*, a friendship that was uniquely the result of her personal encounter with the text through the emotions and memories elicited as she said them. In creating a Titania whose honour among women was paramount, Haring's Titania was more than a comic foil to Oberon's outlandish trick. She was bound by honour and reciprocity to the mother of the child she agreed to raise as her own. Like her fairy court, Haring's Titania was of the earth. Her bower was an enormous hammock made from jute webbing strewn with leaves and tied between two pines, slightly upstage left of the playing space. Each fairy individualized her own costume with the guidance of costume designer Kiki Smith. There was little money that first year, so Smith found an innovative way to create the fairies' benevolent, preternatural sound. The actors playing the fairies 'hammered old spoons flat and drilled holes in them to make necklaces that created a subtle silvery tinkling as they moved', lit by spotlights hung high on the pines (Smith 2021). The audience heard this delicate haunting sound as the fairies moved through the woods illuminated by the light filtering down through the trees.

Set designer Bill Ballou created the lighting effects: 'I got to know those trees intimately because I spent a lot of time climbing them ... I would throw a rope over a sturdy limb and climb up, screwing rented stage lights in the trees and running the cables down ... We also had lights on the ground illuminating the trees from below' (Ballou 2022). His bedroom in the main house served as his office and control booth as well: 'We were shining lights out the windows – doing whatever we could to get the light where it needed to go. It was about learning this whole new environment and having a lot of fun with it' (Ballou 2022). The lighting was integral to the magic: 'For "now the hungry lion roars" at the end of Act V, Puck was discovered on The Mount's highest balcony, pinpointed by a spotlight that made him seem airborne, while the fairies, one by one, lit candles in each window of the house' (Salsbury 1979: 178).

If the fairies were elemental creatures, Oberon and Puck might have emerged from the primordial soup of New York

City's East Village. Gregory Uel Cole's tall and agile Black Oberon wore long black pants open on the sides, loosely laced. He completed the look with leather straps around his bare chest and arms. Tony Simotes, white, compact and muscular, donned flowy culottes in mirrored fabric that shimmered as he moved. Simotes was 'a reluctant Puck' (Simotes 2021). When Packer asked him to play Puck, as he recalled, 'I was very unhappy about it because I had just seen an off-Broadway production of the play and Puck was a ballet dancer, and I thought, I don't want to play a fairy. And that actually became the basis of my character. I was the reluctant fairy, very much of the earth' (2021). Packer believes that audiences respond when actors don't try to hide who they are or what they feel, but instead find a way to use these elements in performance. As it turned out, the casting 'was a match made in heaven', Simotes continued, because he and Cole knew each other from New York University where they were both in the theatre programme (Simotes 2021). Accordingly, their affect was very New York. Susie Fugle, one of the fairies, described their routine as, 'a bit cheeky at times' with the verse (2022). When Oberon ordered Puck, 'About the wood, go swifter than the wind / And Helena of Athens look thou find' (3.2.94–95), Puck responded in a stereotypical New York accent, not moving: 'I *go*, I *go*, *look how* I *go*' (3.2.100). Then 'he wandered off slowly, with his recalcitrant attitude. It was hysterical. They made that relationship alive and real' (Fugle 2022). The pair signalled their invisibility with 'a "musical statues" routine, bodies frozen, eyes darting with comic glee or exasperation' (Salsbury 1979: 177–8; Figure 2).

If Oberon and Puck were New York City cool cats, the rude mechanicals were diligent thespians, roles developed by the young group of actors playing the workman, first through *dropping in* with Packer and Linklater and then with Dennis Krausnick, who used improvisation to guide them through an exploration of their trades. As John Hadden who played Flute / Thisbe explained:

FIGURE 2 *Ensemble: Oberon (Gregory Uel Cole), Fairy (Noni Pratt), Bottom (Jonathan Rutledge), Titania (Andrea Haring), Puck (Tony Simotes), Fairy (Susie Fugle), Fairy (Natsuko Ohama) and Fairy (Gina Weiss). Photo: Warren D. Fowler © F Scott Fowler. Reproduced courtesy of F. Scott Fowler.*

The whole effort was for us to have a sense of the reality of who these characters are and respect for their trades: Rather than Bottom the Weaver being simply a joke, and a slightly derogatory joke as well, we considered what he actually does in the context of Elizabethan life. This was my introduction to how much you can find in a small role and the comic gain you can get from playing it dead real right down the middle ... What's funny with the comic characters is the intensity of their commitment to stakes that are not that consequential, even though to the character they are enormously consequential. It's both funny and sad at the same time. (2022)

Hadden's Flute, the bellows mender, who spoke his part all at once, cues and all, was a tall, lithe Thisbe in a summery yellow dress over his work boots with his blond hair in a top knot. Having hoped his role would be that of a wandering knight, he found a way to be courageous in his womanly garb, becoming more and more irked by the courtly audience's interruptions: 'He was the rebellious one, who spoke truth to power' (Hadden 2022).

The athletic exuberance of the ensemble was the work of youth under the fight direction of B. H. Barry, who created vigorous, stunning arrangements between the lovers that developed the story through movement: he 'had his actors flying through the air and hitting the ground with breathtaking regularity' (Salsbury 1979: 178). The dances, choreographed by John Broome, helped to tell the story of the play. He created a rousing Bergomask for the rude mechanicals and a poignant dance for the rapprochement of Titania and Oberon. The reviewer wrote that the production was 'the best theatrical experience I have had for a very long time, a real treat for people of all ages' (Salsbury 1979: 177).

The play's success was a testament to Packer's vision, steady hand and ability to gather and inspire creative, committed artists. The company had occupied their new home only two months earlier, on 22 May 1978. During those two months, company members established a community that lived, cooked and ate their meals in the house as they worked, trained and rehearsed together on the estate. Packer, together with her co-founders, assembled the company's cast and crew from her former colleagues at the Royal Shakespeare Company; participants from her Ford-funded experimental company; recent graduates of New York University's theatre programme whom Linklater taught, and recent graduates of the Five College Consortium where both Linklater and Packer had recently taught and directed.[2] Susie Fugle, a graduate of London Academy of Music and Drama (LAMDA) who lived in the Berkshires, found her way to the company through word of mouth:

I tracked Tina down and she told me what her vision was … so I went and found this amazing community of people who had passion, not only for the work itself, but for living. It was a deep experience on so many levels. The American actors that came up from New York, Rocco Sisto, Tony Simotes, Kevin Coleman, Gregory Cole, and Kaia Calhoun, were sort of swashbuckling, in that savvy, New York way. And Tina brought in her two pals from the U.K., Gillian Barge and Lorna Heilbron. Tina managed to stride easily among these nationalities … And somehow made it all come together … It was borderless. It wasn't about having an English accent. It wasn't about nationality or race or ethnicity. It was, what do you bring? (2022)

The seeming ease with which the cast inhabited the natural setting emerged from Packer's collaborative rehearsal process guided by master teachers and trainers, including Kristin Linklater for voice, Dennis Krausnick for text and improvisation, John Broome for movement and dance and B. H. Barry for the fights. The cast gathered at the start of each day's rehearsal to check in with their observations about the play. The first two weeks of rehearsal, Packer and Linklater led *dropping in* of the entire play, followed by three weeks of scene rehearsal, broken down by beats, in rotation with in-depth text work, improvisation, movement, fight, dance and voice. This phase was followed by a 'stumble through' of the entire play, several more run-throughs, followed by tech and opening night.

A Midsummer Night's Dream enfolds three worlds: fairies evoking Elizabethan lore, English aristocrats hailing from ancient Athens and sixteenth-century tradesmen carried away by the challenge and joy of putting on a play. By the end the worlds have come together: their 'incongruities, anachronisms, contradictions, and impossible juxtapositions … [are reduced] to a harmony' (Goddard 1951: 76). Similarly, Packer assembled her cast and crew by bringing together people from different worlds, translating them, as it were, into her dream: a community, living, training and performing together at The Mount.

The success of the opening production caused word spread that there was new, lively theatre company in the Berkshires, so Packer mounted two mainstage productions in repertory for the 1979 summer season: *Romeo and Juliet*, directed by Dennis Krausnick and *The Winter's Tale*, directed by Packer. The casts for these productions were international and multicultural, comprised of American, Canadian and British actors. They included the British actor Joseph Marcell (Camillo, who also played Capulet), originally from Santa Lucia, and Gregory Uel Cole (Autolycus/Tybalt), an exceptionally versatile actor and company member who was Black, Kaia Calhoun (Dorcas/Nurse), a company member who is Black, along with established British actors Gillian Barge (Paulina) and Lorna Heilbron (Hermione), and Susie Fugle, a company member (Mopsa). Packer had strong American actors in the leading roles of Polixenes (Eric Booth) and Leontes (Barry Primus), as well as talented younger company members Rocco Sisto (Young Shepherd/Friar Lawrence) and Michael Hammond (Florizel/Benvolio). *The Winter's Tale*, particularly the final scene, garnered praise from reviewers:

> The statue scene was not a piece of clunking dramatic machinery but a metaphor for the notion that romantic artifice and dramatic reality are two sides of a single vision. Gillian Barge had built her Paulina of words medicinal – both healing and pestilential – so that she had become not only a woman who would not stumble, but also one with authority to say 'It is required / You do awake your faith' and make it binding on every heart within earshot. But it was not Barge alone that made it work: it was, too, the breathless two-beat wait after her line, and then the depiction, by the cast, of people impelled to their knees by an over-powering emotion. (Littlefield and Maclean 1980: 182)

After only two seasons, Shakespeare & Company was dubbed 'the glory of this region' (Littlefield 1981: 188). Packer recalled, 'directing *The Winter's Tale* helped me understand in a deep way my role in the company' (2020c). Paulina's unique blend of authority and compassion is itself a form of art, an art she uses to guide the court of Sicilia towards reconciliation: 'Paulina brings the dead statue back to life, which, on a symbolic level is the essence of art itself. In the act of creating, through an act of will, you bring something that was unconscious or inert into consciousness, into flesh and blood' (2020c). The promise of reconciliation embodied in the scene has sustained Packer for over forty-six years (at this writing) through success and the inevitable challenges of being at the helm of a theatre company. Productions don't always come together in time; nevertheless, the actors, some of them on stage in a professional production for the first time, gain experience while working collaboratively and deeply under Packer's direction.

Freedom and loneliness: *The Tempest*, 1980

Tina Packer's 1980 production of *The Tempest* opened with a deafening crack of thunder, prompting the audience to enter the play's world with a physical shift from their blankets on the lawn, 'turning 180°' to 'look up toward the mansion against the dark sky' (Erickson 1981: 189). There they could spy 'Ariel's distant silhouette perched on a tiny platform at the very top of the roof of the mansion as he raised and orchestrated the storm (in conjunction with the sound system) with beautiful abstract gestures' (Erickson 1981: 189). Below, the foundering ship was evoked by an enormous sail covering the terrace, swinging to and fro as if buffeted by the storm, while mariners fell from ratlines to the thunderous 'sound of a ship breaking up on the rocks' (Eckert 1980). Packer recalled with pleasure the ingenuity of her artistic team, noting that the 'cracking of the ship in two filled the whole space, brilliantly realistic and frightening' (2023a). The spectacular scene was the work of sound engineer Roger Reynolds and set designer Bill Ballou along with a youthful, fearless cast. Through his contacts in New York City, Ballou acquired 'a huge amount of the synthetic gauze that Francis Hines had used to wrap the Washington Square Monument ... It was the perfect material because it would float like a sail, but the wind went through it' (2022). His crew sewed together strips of the gauze to make the sail, and 'carved down a huge cedar log for the boom' (Ballou 2022). They built the ratlines out of rope, attaching them to the fire escapes on the third story of the house above the terrace, and covered the concrete floor of the terrace with crash mats: 'For the storm, we had someone manipulating the boom, sending the sail back and forth, and people climbing the ropes, swinging, then falling [onto the crash mats] during the storm' (Ballou 2022). The storm stopped on cue when Harris Yulin's Prospero tapped the ground with his staff, cueing the audience to shift back in their seats, discovering him centre stage at the base of the natural amphitheatre where he was attempting to calm his daughter, Caris Corfman's Miranda. Instantly, the special effects gave way to the unmediated vibrations of the human voice: 'Any production of Shakespeare's *The Tempest* needs to decide where it stands on the scale between human emotion and theatrical magic. Director Tina Packer has successfully opted for the human dynamic ... [T]he words and the emotions that the words convey are the crucial elements of the drama' (Gates 1981: 116).

Packer used the natural setting surrounding the mainstage to immerse the audience in the play's world:

> Prospero's cell was the plain, multi-level wooden stage. Adjacent to this was a grove of pines, in front of which an area carpeted with needles became in effect a second stage. From here, a path used as one of a seemingly infinite variety of entrances and exits led up to the Edith Wharton mansion. The overall effect was that the audience was environed by the action. (Erickson 1981: 189)

Reynolds complemented the staging with compositions and aural effects that enveloped the audience with the isle's noises, sounds and sweet airs. Ballou had spent the past two summers enhancing the set and upgrading his lighting equipment. Their combined artistry deepened the audience's connection to the story: 'The sound system spreads in almost a complete circle around the audience. The lights are hidden in trees as well as hung on huge poles. The infinite variety of moods captured among the trees and on that versatile stage all work together to let an audience fill in with its own imaginings, the specifics of locale and setting' (Eckert 1980).

While the spectacle of the shipwreck occurred above and behind the audience, the shock of Caliban's entrance occurred below. As Joe Morton, who played Caliban, recalled,

> There was an existing hole right under the apex of the stage that led underneath. When I saw that hole, I knew that was where I wanted to make my entrance. Tina thought it was a great idea; so, I emerged from this hole, right in front of the audience, especially those close to the stage near the bottom of the slope. At first, all they could see was something dark and slithering. I used charcoal so that my body was almost pitch black. Every night there was a gasp of terror. They didn't know what I was, which was exactly the response that we wanted. After that I would turn and slither up onto the stage. (2022)

The alarm and ambiguity of Caliban's entrance was emblematic of Morton's characterization. He was eloquent in manifesting his character's love of the isle with unique noises that complemented Shakespeare's verse: 'His large hands [created by wearing oversized gloves] were used in emphatic gestures – a vertical clapping or a pounding of the fist on his bare chest – to punctuate verbal points. An assortment of convincing groans and growls served as background, imbuing his language with striking visceral impact' (Erickson 1981: 189). For his speeches, he pronounced each word carefully, 'as if language was still an awkward instrument' (Erickson 1981: 189). Morton's Caliban was also vigorously athletic. He slithered, tumbled, walked upright, sometimes he bent at the waist or crouched, as if on hind legs, in an 'animal-like posture' (Erickson 1981: 189). Yet his costume included a pointed departure from the oft used technique of costuming Caliban with a large fin or tail simply because Trinculo, Antonio and Sebastian mockingly refer to him as a fish. Morton donned a tribal accoutrement made of leather and fur around his waist: 'it spread out into a train so that it looked like a tail' (Morton 2022). Morton recalled that he did 'a lot more research' for this production, his second as Caliban: 'I found some wonderful books on different African tribes, so the makeup I used was Aboriginal, from an African tribe' (2022).[3] His overall appearance evoked aboriginal tribal standing, developed in consultation with Kiki Smith the designer. He masked his body with charcoal, making it appear as black as pitch, applying ochre to his face to create a lighter brown mask while leaving 'large circles around his eyes to highlight their expressiveness' (Erickson 1981: 189). He streaked his hair with 'a paste of flour and water' and the crowning touch, he recalled, was comprised of 'white feathers strewn into my hair across the top of my head' (Morton 2022). Morton played Caliban in the way he understood him from *dropping in*, as both 'creature' and 'human' in a 'world where you've got fairies and magic and all the rest of it' (2022). He noted that when Miranda first meets Ferdinand, she refers to him as 'the third man that e'er I saw' (1.2.449) thereby implying that Caliban was the second.

One reviewer wrote that Morton 'gets across all the implications and inferences of the role – the native deprived of his land, the slave and the master, the animal who yearns to ravage the beauty that is placed before him. It is all intermixed perfectly; a Caliban on which to model all Calibans' (Bass 1980: 9). Morton saw Caliban's desire differently: 'he was just pursuing what is natural' (2022). The moment is an interesting one because it is an important crux in the play that we hear about after the fact from the opposing sides. This suggests that perhaps the reviewer was taking a bit of license in his review, since it seems he was writing about his knowledge of the play rather than what he experienced in the production. I have similar reservations about the repetition of 'monster' and 'monstrous' in other reviews I cite here. These are the words of the European characters in the play. My sense of Morton's portrayal of Caliban from images printed in the newspaper reviews is that he was far from looking like a monster. Rather, as he described himself, his Caliban appears to have been at once a 'creature' and 'human' (Morton 2022), a human wearing distinguished tribal garb.

Morton found the experience rewarding, noting how, with the cast living and rehearsing together for two months they drew together in a deep embodiment of the play's world:

> It was like a big vacation, but you're working really hard, and at the same time, it's one-hundred percent joyful ... We all took turns cooking in the kitchen, and we'd all have to clean the house, so it was really a commune as much as a theater company. It helped the company to congeal and work as well as it did because we lived together. We weren't just going home after rehearsals every night. You would hear other people rehearsing or walking around the grounds ... It helped us develop our own language amongst one another in terms of the play. (2022)

That language was apparent in the relationship between Ariel and Caliban. Packer departed from the tradition of treating Caliban and Ariel as antagonists or opposites. Neil Sim's lean and lithe Ariel was also Black: 'Though not overstated, a partial overlap and affinity – rather than absolute contrast – with Caliban was suggested by Ariel's demeanor and behavior ... While Mr. Sims's singing was of extraordinary beauty, he also employed a set of cackling, chuckling noises' (Erickson 1981: 189). Joanne Gates noted, 'Sims is more human than sprite. He suffers, stumbles, and once makes the mistake of casting his own spell on himself' (Gates 1981: 117). These earthier qualities and his painful desire for freedom aligned Sim's Ariel with Caliban. Both were accomplished singers, and both wore loincloths that, especially in the case of Ariel, 'kept the audience aware of his physical presence' even when he wasn't speaking (Erickson 1981: 189). In a telling moment, 'Caliban interrupted the singing of Stephano and Trinculo with his insistent "That's not the tune," and then listened intently to Ariel's exquisite version' (Erickson 1981: 189). Caliban's sensitivity to music, not only his love of the sounds of the isle but also here, in direct contrast to Stephano and Trinculo, indicated his innate sensitivity and his growing awareness of his newfound comrades' shortcomings. Their comic scenes earned plaudits:

> Most impressive were Joe Morton as Caliban and Rocco Sisto as Trinculo. The former character was monstrous [again, at least in the words of this reviewer] yet touching, supremely petty yet with flashes of true dignity. The latter gave us a masterful interpretation of a Shakespearian clown – all surface mirth with flashes of disturbing poignancy throughout … Miss Packer is not a gimmicky director. She has clearly pondered and absorbed this play, in overall theme as well as in specific detail. The wit and sparkle of the Caliban, Trinculo, Stephano scenes have rarely seemed more acute and accurate. (Eckert 1980: 11)

Morton recalled that for the freedom song with Trinculo and Stephano he performed 'wonderful back flips' (Morton 2022). Joanne Gates thought that Caliban's 'conversion from cowering monster to liquor-inspired songster' was 'the best scene in the production', observing that his singing of the freedom lyric 'clos[ed] the first act with a well-deserved ovation' (1981: 117).

Packer's casting, combined with her direction of Caliban and Ariel, resulted in a colonial interpretation of *The Tempest* that embodied a more general comment on power and oppression. Terry Fox of *The Village Voice* made note of Packer's casting, pointing out that because Stephano was played by a Black actor, Gregory Uel Cole, 'The servant who comes upon a captive monster, and, in the name of freedom, makes the monster his own slave, is not just a fool but a representative of the unending chain of power society provides' (Fox 1980).[4]

The relationship between Morton's Caliban and Yulin's Prospero was complex, a complexity they found in the text through *dropping in*: on the one hand they had become antagonists, yet within that antagonism was a sense that they were also a family. As Gates wrote, Yulin 'shows the change from manipulating revenger to forgiving parent, brother and master with a delicate, sometimes troubled, sensitivity' (1981: 116). As well, she remarked on the clarity of the production's storytelling: 'through all the multitude of plots, of lost and drunken parties, and attempts at mutiny, we never lose sight of Prospero's complex tale of his disfranchisement' (1981: 116). Prospero's disenfranchisement ironically mirrors Caliban's, and in this production that irony was given another twist by the casting. In addition to Caliban, Ariel and Stephano, the King of Naples and Adrian were played by Black actors, resulting in a tense moment when the production's white Sebastian blamed the Black King Alonso for the shipwreck because he 'loos[ed] his daughter to an African', rather than 'bless our Europe with your daughter' (2.1.124–125). This detail added a complex dimension to the production's portrayal of colonialism, since the character in the production with the most political power was Black. It also prompted a reflection on what Caliban might have been or might become (Figure 3).[5]

At the heart of this entanglement of race, politics, ambition and greed was the production's focus on the tension between freedom and loneliness: 'everyone is looking for their freedom. They get it very different ways' (Morton 2022). As Morton explained, his Caliban held opposing ideas and feelings about Prospero: 'He looked at Prospero as a usurper: here was a creature who had stolen the island from him, and he was willing to kill him to get it back' (2022). Yet, 'as far as Caliban, Ariel, Miranda and Prospero are concerned, they

FIGURE 3 *Ensemble: King of Naples (Herb Davis), Francisco (Brian Varga), Adrian (Garfield Randelman), Antonio (Kevin Coleman), Sebastian (David Breithbarth) and Gonzalo (Tom Kunis). Photo: Warren D. Fowler © F Scott Fowler. Reproduced courtesy of F. Scott Fowler.*

are a family. It's dysfunctional, but it's the only family he has, and at the end – suddenly, everyone is gone … that's the irony of the play. Yes, he gets his island back, but not the way he wanted. He felt abandoned' (2022). He was free, but completely alone.

Yulin's performance of the epilogue crystallized the play's complexities into the central conflict between the need for connection and the desire for freedom. He stood facing the audience from the same spot where he had allayed the storm with a tap of his staff: 'Yulin compressed Prospero's awareness of his need for "pardon" into the final phrase "set me free," which he spoke with an urgent, rising voice that recapitulated previously stressed allusions to freedom – especially Caliban's' (Erickson 1981: 190). Both Prospero and Caliban were utterly alone at the end. Caliban was free, but desolate. Prospero realized only death would set him free. His magic had failed to change his brother Antonio, who remained without compassion or remorse while his 'creature' his 'thing of darkness' proved to be more humane than the lot, uttering with simple dignity his final line, 'I will be wise hereafter and seek for grace'. From this vantage point, the production is an aching meditation on our collective history.

Coming of age in Illyria: *Twelfth Night*, 1981–82

For the company's fourth summer season in 1981, Packer continued to explore multicultural casting in *As You Like It* and *Twelfth Night*. Company members performed in repertory while training in voice, movement, fight, text and clown with master teachers Kristin Linklater, John Broome, B. H. Barry, Neil Freeman and Merry Conway. The production of *As You Like It* delighted audiences: 'When Hymen appeared through the trees to solemn music, a rapt audience didn't even notice that the rain had begun. And the knee-slapping dance with which the whole company ended the play was so good that it actually stopped the rain from falling' (Berek 1982: 213). Gregory Uel Cole, who is Black, played Jaques in *As You Like It* and Orsino in *Twelfth Night* while Kaia Calhoun, who is Black, played Phebe in *As You Like It* and Olivia in *Twelfth Night*. Packer cast her near look-alike white actors, Gregory Johnson and Virginia Ness, as Sebastian and Viola for *Twelfth Night*. *The New York Times* announcement for the play's opening in Prospect Park described the company as 'interracial', perhaps because the production ended with two 'interracial' couples (Shepard 1982: C16). In a subsequent feature article the writer observed, 'the single most American aspect of Shakespeare & Company is its racial mix', quoting Gregory Uel Cole who noted dryly, 'I've been given the opportunity to play roles I wouldn't be able to play elsewhere … Socially, it's wonderful to see a black actor perform Shakespeare because audiences think blacks can't speak

English' (Anderson 1982: C15). Virginia Ness and Kaia Calhoun were praised for their performances at different times during the play's run. In Canada, where the production opened at the *Onstage 81* international festival in Toronto Canada, the reviewer wrote: 'Ness has so much personality, of an insolent and frolicsome nature, that she flooded the stage with an effervescent fizz whenever she appeared' (R. C. 1981). A year later, when the production played in Prospect Park, Brooklyn, Calhoun's Olivia was highlighted as the most 'spirited' of the two leading ladies (Dunning 1982: L40). Kristin Linklater garnered praise for her Maria: 'what she gives, apart from the endless vocal nuance, is a deeply felt sense of the character: a plain woman endowed with cleverness, who has finally summoned the nerve to take revenge on poor Malvolio' (R. C. 1981). Packer's directing was 'well-paced and confident' (R. C. 1981) and 'perfectly balanced the play's romance and comedy, the latter with wonderfully restrained slapstick, the former without a trace of standard coyness' (Kelly 1981: 49).

Twelfth Night's songs are intrinsic to the play's dramatic sensibility (Walker 1994: 222). The characters' emotions are in symbiotic relationship with the play's weather, as indicated by the play's closing ditty. Accordingly, for the mise en scène, Packer made the production's music and sound an extension of the landscape: 'Lights flood down through the trees, music sweeps up from the distance of the forest as ambling musicians casually establish themselves on a square of flooring near the stage' (Kelly 1981: 51). The integration of the music and sound with the setting was the work of Bruce Odland, who specializes in writing compositions that harmonize with natural environments. Odland built original instruments for the Illyrian world. The first was dubbed a 'sortative' because it was 'sort of' like a 'portative', the small portable pipe organ originating in Italy during the Trecento (Coffin 2023). The second, mounted on a large tree near the musicians, was a 'tree harp', comprised of eight piano strings with a contact microphone to create sound effects. The tree itself appeared to thunder, screech and whistle in response to the unfolding events. An assortment of gemshorns and recorders added texture, atmosphere and dimension to the songs (Coffin 2023).

Feste, whose songs are the fulcrum of the play's comic and tragic contours, was deftly played by John Hadden:

> Garbed in subdued colors and with a deaths-head for a bauble, Hadden admirably acknowledged Feste's dark side, showing that the clown, along with Maria, is one of the few characters in the play not blinded by love or self-absorption. But Hadden's Feste was also funny; moments when Olivia and Orsino failed to laugh reflected badly on them rather than on the Clown. (Berek 1982: 213)

The reviewer for *The New York Times* remarked that Hadden was 'surprisingly young and handsome for a Feste' who nevertheless was successful at 'incorporat[ing] the play of folly and wisdom that is a signature theme of "Twelfth Night." Capable of jolting cruelty, he is a figure of interchangeable sweetness and melancholy' (Dunning 1982). The production's youthful Feste was by design. One of the play's central themes is that 'Youth's a stuff will not endure', the final line of 'O Mistress Mine' which Feste sings in act 2 scene 3. Packer's concept for the production was inspired by this idea, so everyone in her Illyria was youthful except Sir Toby and Maria. The rehearsal process, particularly *dropping in* and improvisation, created personal stakes for the characters, especially Hadden's Feste and Rocco Sisto's Malvolio, the play's central antagonists and clowns. In the first two weeks of rehearsal during *dropping in* Kaia Calhoun's Olivia, Hadden's Feste and Sisto's Malvolio discovered through the text how well the characters know each other, creating the sense among them that they all grew up together. As Hadden recalled, he and Calhoun's Olivia were especially close:

> We had a long history and found that we had grown up taking lessons together with Olivia's brother from her father and Toby, who hadn't gone to seed yet, and we would all laugh together, with Feste being the oddball, and it was only class that prevented us [Feste and Olivia] from being a natural match. There is so much sadness over love in his songs, she understands him better than anyone else, and she is furious with him for abandoning her after the deaths of her father and brother. (2023)

These emotional underpinnings of the plot developed personal stakes for the actors, adding yet another young man – Feste – to the orbit of Olivia's would-be wooers. Yet Hadden's Feste, knew he had no chance with her because of their difference in social status (2023). In a younger Feste's contained desire for Olivia, then, Virginia Ness's Viola/Cesario became his refracted mirror. They understood one another as they sized each other up in their central scene together, 3.1, when Feste implies that Cesario is Orsino's 'fool' (3.1.38). Meanwhile, as Hadden pointed out, his rivalry with Rocco Sisto's Malvolio was long-standing, going all the way back to childhood. Hadden recalled: 'We were mates in this little world of Olivia's and her father's household. We realised we'd known each other from childhood, so there's a lot of history that we found in the rehearsal process. Without that history, then it's just someone you dislike and that doesn't go anywhere on stage. There has to be a cost' (2021). The cost for them began long before the game of revenge that unfolds in the play. Hadden felt that he and Malvolio had been rivals for Olivia's affection since childhood. Thus, the three actors felt there was a much longer history behind the moment when Sisto's Malvolio called Hadden's Feste 'a barren rascal' in front of Olivia, thereby inciting Feste's desire for revenge (1.5.71–2). These stakes are for the actors to discover and develop through the process of rehearsal rather than a reading of the play that the audience is meant to ascertain. What does reach the audience, however, through the actors' voices is the intensity of emotion indicating that the stakes are high. As shown here, it is through the process of *dropping in* the text that the actors create their characters' relationships and memories, deeply grounding them in their psyches in a way that resonates in their voices. As Hadden explained, in the lead up to that moment, when his Feste returns after vanishing unaccountably, he had to compete yet again with Malvolio to get back in Olivia's good graces, as he had done all the while growing up:

> The stooge Malvolio loves keeping her in mourning. And here comes the fool whom she grew up with, who has been gone for six months after her brother died. He disappeared when she needed him most. And he isn't funny anymore … But then he is called on to do it, or else hang in front of Malvolio, who hates him. (2021)

Their long history also raised the stakes for Kaia Calhoun's Olivia, who was furious with Hadden's Feste. Linklater's Maria, who was also older than Feste, admonished him that he must make his excuse wisely to avoid hanging (1.5.71–2). Olivia was still so angry with him that she ordered him taken away immediately (1.5.34). Hadden explained that his Feste was in what is referred to in clown training at Shakespeare & Company as 'the drop' (2021). He was completely humiliated in front of the woman he has loved since childhood and his gloating archnemesis. An important aspect of clown training at the company is that the clown must be able to find the game in any situation. Anything can become a game. The clown must be observant, open and flexible enough to ascertain where the game might exist in a serious situation and then turn it around.[6] The dialogue between Olivia and Feste is written in such a way that it shows how Feste keeps the game going in order to get back into Olivia's good graces. For Hadden, Feste's most daring moment was when he told Olivia her brother was in hell. He was encouraged to go that far, when in his previous exchange, he took the chance of making an aural pun while declaring that he was wrongfully arrested, as he stood, held between the two guards primed to haul him offstage: 'Misprision in the highest degree!' he shouted, moving on rapidly he spoke the Latin, '*Cucullus non facit monacum*', (the cowl doesn't make the priest), (1.5.50–52), emphasizing the hard 'k' sound in '*facit*'. The moment would elicit a collective gasp from the audience quickly followed by laughter (Hadden 2022). By this time in their exchange, Calhoun's Olivia had guardedly joined the game. Having made it past the aural pun, Hadden's Feste went further, daring to insult her in order to shake her out of her mourning. Because Hadden's Feste had loved Olivia since childhood, he was willing to put his life on the line to shake her out of her mourning: 'This is the moment. He has to risk his life for her for real so that she can hear him. He's on the floor with nothing. He has to be audacious to shake her from her sorrow' (Hadden 2022). Hadden's Feste, dared to say, '*I think his soul is in hell, Madonna*' (1.5.63). Calhoun's Olivia retorted 'I *know* his soul is in heaven, *fool*' (1.5.65), setting Hadden's Feste up to cinch his point, 'The more fool, Madonna, to mourn for your brother's soul being in Heaven. Take away the fool, gentlemen', he quipped, nodding at Calhoun's Olivia. As Hadden pointed out, 'Playing the fool is a series of those moments all the way through. He's on a high wire the whole time' (Hadden 2022).

Feste's submerged feelings for Olivia created a further contrast with Malvolio, whose designs on Olivia stemmed solely from the hope of advancing his status, while the rivalry between Hadden's Feste and Sisto's Malvolio was fierce. The result was an unsympathetic, if young, Malvolio. He was so successful in creating a youthful 'teetering tower of leering self-importance', as one reviewer noted (R. C. 1981), that another reviewer saw it as a flaw in the performance: 'it's difficult to be compassionate about him within the cruelty of his final ridicule' (Kelly 1981: 51). As Sisto pointed out, Malvolio is misshapen at the level of his speech: 'Neil Freeman (the company's First Folio Text expert) showed me that his prose is misshapen. He can't enter into that beautiful realm of verse completion where Viola and Olivia live' (Sisto 2022). His language was not 'simpatico' with anyone in the play (Sisto 2022). In the box-tree scene (2.5.13–168), Sisto explained, 'I felt even more in love with myself. I was walking around in front of my mistress in an incredibly beautiful outfit, in the height of fashion, and I *knew* that she that loved to look at me' (Sisto 2022). Sisto noted that when Malvolio says he is 'playing with some rich jewel' (2.5.57), it shows how 'masturbatory' he is, as his jewel is located on an imaginary codpiece, an emblem for his self-love. When Sisto's Malvolio was reading the letter and launched into his aria, 'some are born great' (2.5.135–6), Packer cued the sound of thunder from Odland's tree harp, a warning, perhaps from Jove himself.

Packer's cast had a middle-aged Maria, played by Kristin Linklater, creating the prank on the younger Malvolio as if to teach him a lesson while having a good bit of fun at his expense and winning the heart of Sir Toby, who was also played by middle-aged actors (Paul Massie and subsequently Larry Block). For the 'Sir Topaz' scene (4.2), Malvolio was locked in a large shipping crate. The audience could hear but not see him. Usually when productions create a sympathetic Malvolio, the audience is privy to his suffering. Sisto did not want to play Malvolio for sympathy in this scene, feeling that the text shows he retains his sense that he is above everyone, as indicated by his repeated promises of a reward to Feste, as if he were more than a steward, a servant in Olivia's household. Sisto recalled that 'during the Topaz scene, my whole costume and make-up were deconstructed', so that when he emerged from inside the crate, 'I looked like Heath Ledger in *The Dark Knight*' (Sisto 2022). He remained angry and indignant as he accused Olivia of having done him 'notorious wrong' (5.1.318–319). He 'railed at everyone and went into a complete tizzy' (Sisto 2022), and when he shouted, 'I will be revenged on the whole pack of you' (5.1.368), the thunder clapped again, at which point he thought, 'oh sh—t' and exited: 'that was the drop for him – when the thunder came in' (Sisto 2022). Having left the stage, he evaded the experience of public shame.

On playing the role, Sisto recalled, 'It was a challenge for me to be that vicious going up against Kristin [Linklater], who played his antagonist, Maria' (Sisto 2022). He had been her student in the acting programme at New York University and was now an actor in the company she co-founded with Packer. He found that 'being a clown allowed me to do that. I was able to let loose. We did a lot of improvising with respect to status and arrogance' (Sisto 2022). Kevin Coleman also recalled how helpful the clown training was:

> We had gone through a lot of clown training. The clown work with Merry Conway made a huge difference in rehearsal because it became really clear that the clown works by being raw – not trying to be funny. As soon as you try to be funny, the audience knows it immediately and resents it. What is required of the clown is openness, a willingness to be vulnerable, to be hurt, and to get yourself back up off the floor and move on. I'd say clown is the soul of the actor. Clown reveals humanity moment by moment at our best and our worst. That's when theater becomes illuminating, rather than merely dramatic or entertaining. (Coleman 2022a)

Having clowns who were the same age as the romantic leads complicated the romantic plots while illuminating the clowns in Viola, Olivia and Orsino, who also were exposed and humiliated, albeit more gently. Calhoun's Olivia fell in love with a woman, Ness's Viola, had inadvertently made a woman fall in love with her. Gregory Cole's Orsino appeared ridiculous to the audience when he declared 'no woman's sides / Can bide the beating of so strong a passion / As love doth give my heart' (2.4.92–94). Ironically, Ness's Viola showed that she was stronger than he was in her unspoken love for him. Some believe that people love us for our clown, the aspects of ourselves we reveal unawares.[7] From this perspective, the play is full of clowns. Liviu Ciulei ran with this idea in his concept for his Guthrie Theater production of *Twelfth Night* three years later in 1984, set in an enormous circus tent. Each character was 'attired in terms of circus proper or related forms from commedia dell'arte to Woody Allen' (Clayton 1985: 356).[8]

Kevin Coleman, one of the company's most skilled and long-standing clowns, recalled that his Andrew Aguecheek 'was a very unathletic person, and I had to be really athletic to make him that way' (2022a). He wore maroon leatherette football padding on his elbows, knees and shoulders, as well padding on his forehead because he kept running into the trees: 'I was very happy to just play wild and extreme. My first entrance was to come in, trip, fall, and roll down the stairs. The audience would gasp because it looked really painful. Then I'd quickly stand up as if it was business as usual for that character' (2022a). Coleman's character was noted for his flexibility: 'Aguecheek moved as if he'd had latex injections in every limb, an effect heightened by the delightful idea of having gloves hanging by strings from his wrists and flopping with every gesture' (R. C. 1981).

Amid his antic pratfalls, Coleman experienced a poignant moment that taught him to play the line straight, connecting with a personal sense of loss: 'Andrew has the sweetest line – "I was adored once too" – When I said that I could feel the audience connect with me. I realised I had to be vulnerable and surrender to that line because of its poignancy – playing it flippantly or trying to be funny with it was completely wrong for the moment' (2022a). The line is near the end of the 'cakes and ale' scene (2.3) in response to Sir Toby's remark that Maria's 'a beagle true bred, and one that adores me. What o' that?' (2.3.67–68). As foolish as Aguecheek was, however, his poignant delivery of the line showed Sir Toby for the selfish drunken wastrel that he was. The moment suggested that Sir Toby and Malvolio, like the play's comedy and tragedy, youth and age, might be two sides of the same coin.

Packer's casting, with youthful actors in the roles of Feste and Malvolio, combined with *dropping in*, created a production that was a coming-of-age journey not only for Viola, Olivia, Sebastian and Orsino but also for Feste and Malvolio, with only Maria and Sir Toby as representatives of an older generation hardly up to the task of providing adult guidance and wisdom. In Packer's view Orsino is the barometer of the play's weather: 'The play begins with Orsino's self-absorption and ends with his concern for others, as indicated in his final line when he sends someone after Malvolio to bring him back into the fold' (2021b). Orsino's arc requires a versatile actor, one who can be narcissistic and ridiculous while evolving into someone who is wise and generous. Gregory Uel Cole, who previously played Oberon and Stephano, while playing Jaques that same summer, ably navigated the role, as the reviewer for the *Toronto Star* wrote: 'He's long lean and languorous … Every word is given due weight and thoughtfully delivered. There's no sense of hurry. Even the pauses are given due weight. And that sets the tone for the whole performance of *Twelfth Night*' (Crew 1981: Arts 3).

For Packer the play moves from a scattering of individuals focussed on their own sorrows towards community, a community that has undergone an uncomfortable awakening and is now more clear-eyed. The production's closing moments indicated this arc with tweak of the final scene. In the scene as written and often performed, Feste is alone on stage to sing the closing song, 'When that I was and a tiny little boy'. Because the song's tune and words are melancholy, many productions will segue into a jig after the song, bringing the couples back on stage to dance joyfully prior to curtain. In contrast, Packer ended her production with all the characters slowly joining Feste in his melancholy song: 'Feste began to sing of the wind and the rain' with the two young couples remaining on stage. Then gradually, 'the rest of the cast assembled with the lovers and joined in Feste's song, thereby acknowledging, as it were, both the allure of love's magic community and the threat to that community from time and change' (Berek 1982: 213). Sisto's Malvolio returned to join the singing as well, a movement that echoed Feste's earlier departure and return, implying that, with their long history, this has happened before. Packer sees the play as 'very much about this world' in its sober, if wistful exploration of love (2021b). They have all been through the wind and the rain and will continue to bear the changeable weather of their Illyrian world, of which their emotions are very much a part: 'Feste's songs all serve as touchstones by which to measure the emotional state of his listeners. Toby and Andrew wept in sodden sentimentality as they heard "O Mistress mine"; Viola and Curio joined feelingly in the last stanza of "Come Away, Death"' (Berek 1982: 213). The combined effect of returning the cast to the stage and the melancholy nature of the song made the point that, as Packer put it, 'It's a happy ending because people are with those they love, even though they may not live happily ever after' (2021b).

Packer's casting of *Twelfth Night* resulted in an illuminating perspective on the play, while the same approach posed problems for her 1982 *Macbeth*. The reviewers for *The Boston Globe* and *Theatre Journal* agreed that, despite the masterful use of the outdoor space, the actors at the centre of the production, Lorraine Toussant as Lady Macbeth and Timothy Saukiavicus as Macbeth, were 'unusually young' (Engstrom 1982: 23) and therefore 'poorly' cast (Cartelli 1983: 256), as they were not ready for demands of the roles. Engstrom praised Packer's staging, 'which brings the tragedy's grubby physical reality to life', adding that she 'moves her young actors like the very wind in and around the spacious, verdant amphitheater'. Yet, he asked, 'without a compelling Macbeth and Lady Macbeth, what are we all here for?' (1982: 23).

For the next three summers, Packer staged slightly different versions of *The Comedy of Errors*, along with *Romeo and Juliet* in 1984, co-directed with Dennis Krausnick, and *A Midsummer Night's Dream* in 1984, co-directed with Kevin Coleman, performed in repertory at the Prospect Park Bandshell Brooklyn. *The New York Times* reviewer wrote, 'In this lucid, broadly comic production, romance is strictly a game for fools. Acted in the broad, physical style of an adventure movie, this is a "Dream" that should appeal especially to children. But the very literal, unpoetic interpretation of the play is intelligent and consistent enough in its view to engage adults as well' (Holden 1984: C24). Packer's reputation had grown rapidly, and she was becoming increasingly occupied with expanding her company into two locations, one in Boston, in her new position as artistic director of the Boston Shakespeare Company, the other in Lenox at The Mount. The two locations would enable her to have year-round programming while developing both her audience and actor bases in Boston's university and culture rich city. The promise of that opportunity seemed worth a few years of dividing her attention between the two organizations, and eventually seems to have taken its toll on the quality and focus of her productions near the end of the decade. Even so, her highly trained company members delighted audiences and reviewers with successive productions of *The Comedy Errors* between 1983 and 1985. Of the 1983 production, the reviewer noted that it 'went beyond energetic slapstick; the reunions in the end were unabashedly joyous, and the major characters found their mates with such delight that they seemed early examples of the genial couples of Shakespeare's romantic comedies' (Hageman 1984: 222–3). Another noted, 'It isn't often that one can take a voluptuous pleasure in simply hearing the sound of the English language as is the case here. The actors, all young and attractive, read Shakespeare's lines as if no one had ever read them before' (Engstrom 1983: 23). Packer's casting in the 1983 production was singled out as 'daring' by Errol Hill in his groundbreaking book, *Shakespeare in Sable*. In his chapter, 'Toward the Future', he noted that among the cast of nineteen, four were Black actors: 'Two were newly graduated apprentices who had been advanced to full status in the company' a third, was an 'actor of experience ... entrusted with the part of the Duke of Ephesus', and the fourth was Fran Bennett, in the role of the abbess. Her husband, Egeon, was played by Dan Moran, who is white. Their two sons, the Antipholi of Ephesus and Syracuse, were played by white actors Michael Hammond and John Hadden. Hill pointed out that Bennett, a 'Linklater-trained specialist of considerable vocal power' gave 'the Abbess's long speeches a quality of revivalism, reminiscent of black Baptist preachers, that made them distinctive and enjoyable' (Hill 1984b: 185). Bennett's embodiment of the abbess manifested a particular American cultural experience, exemplifying Packer's approach to multicultural Shakespearean theatre. Through the character of the abbess, who is central to the play's resolution, Bennett added to the delight and surprise of the play's reconciliation scene.

In the 1984 mounting of the play one reviewer noticed how the darkness brought out in the opening scene in (extratextual) ill-treatment of Egeon corresponded to that of the beating of the Dromios. As well, he appreciated the 'the fluidity of the playing space' which created 'an impression of spaciousness and a sense that the audience occupies the same territory as the characters' (MacDonald 1986: 109). In 1985, Engstrom enjoyed the production yet again, observing that Packer 'bring[s] out the dark undertones of a comedy that admittedly does contain some pretty scary elements, imminent violent death and loss of identity being only two of them. In her hands the play stands revealed as a rich piece of Rembrandt-like chiaroscuro ... rather than a raucous comic strip in black and white' (Engstrom 1985: 73). Even so, he said it was time for her to move on: 'Of the tragedies [the company] has done only "Romeo and Juliet" and "Macbeth," each its own way, disappointing. Having staked out the foothills so well, isn't it time to start aiming for the heights?' (Engstrom 1985: 73). It's surprising that Engstrom was nudging Packer to try her hand at the tragedies when he had earlier criticized her *Romeo and Juliet* as, perhaps, 'inappropriate for the space' (1984: 67). He had a point, one that Packer understood. The outdoor stage was not congenial to all of Shakespeare's plays. It was, perhaps, more inviting to the physical and mental hijinks of comedy and episodic arcs of the romances.

Antony and Cleopatra is expansive in its geographical reach, shifting between Rome and Egypt, while evoking comedy in the deepest sense at the end when Antony and Cleopatra are joined in the afterlife ('Husband, I come'). Packer's bold conception of the play for her 1986 mainstage summer production was to cast white actors as the Romans and Black actors as the Egyptians. The reviewers were again silent on her use of multicultural casting. They found the performances wanting, but praised Packer's staging:

> the landscape serves both as indoor and outdoor space. Egypt is on stage left, Rome on stage right, and the woods in the middle become the scene of battle. In the distance … a sail is unfurled for the navy at Actium … On a terrace of the Mount, we hear a chorus singing; on a knoll behind us, a horse carries a soldier killed in battle, and, through sidelit trees, we see Antony and Octavius take a political walk in the woods. (Gussow 1986: C18)

Another wrote that the production was 'a brave but inescapably prosaic try', noting that 'Packer moves her sizable company smartly and fills the evening with handsome stage pictures and groupings' (Carr 1986: 10).

For this production Packer partnered with The Cleveland Playhouse. Richard Oberlin, the artistic director, was cast as Anthony, while the much younger Michelle Shay, a company member at the time, who is Black, played Cleopatra. The result was that in fulfilling the concept while supporting her company's financial viability, she compromised her company's ethos. The casting included actors, however experienced, that had not undergone the company's rigorous training programme and therefore did not have the vocal power and physical technique to perform comfortably in the space. This challenge was exacerbated by the exceptionally rainy summer that disrupted rehearsal and performance schedules.

Packer's plan to have an urban base in Boston did not materialize. Even so she closed her first decade with a successful 1987 winter season there. In order to assuage wounds and built trust, at least on this side of the Atlantic, she focussed on Irish playwrights during a time when 'The Troubles' had taken on renewed fervour with the death of Bobby Sands. The

Boston mayor at the time was Raymond Flynn, a Catholic of Irish descent. Out of that foray, she met Jonathan Epstein, who would prove to be among the company's most versatile actors.

Conclusion

Packer's first decade at The Mount was driven by the creative energy of youth, of beginnings and discovery, as the company found ingenious ways to put on a play using the resources available. Company members lived, trained and performed together on Edith Wharton's charming, if weather-beaten estate. They were nurtured and inspired by the natural world that surrounded them. The spruce trees on the property became part of the set and cast. On hot days Kristin Linklater would take cast members to Laurel Lake at the edge of the property where they would stand waist deep in the cool water for vocal warm-ups. They reached out to the community in the first year, teaching in the local schools and hosting their inaugural training workshop the first winter. These activities grew into the company's renowned training and education programs (see Merlin and Packer 2020: 83–236). Packer's productions provided opportunities for newly minted actors to gain experience in their first professional plays. Lorraine Toussaint, who played Lady Macbeth in the 1982 production, is now a well-known actor. In the summer of 2023 Toussant played Gertrude opposite John Douglas Thompson's Claudius in New York City's Shakespeare in the Park production of *Hamlet*. Both actors started their early careers with performances on the outdoor mainstage at The Mount.

Over the course of the decade Packer continued to develop her grand mise en scène style, skillfully immersing the audience in the action using the Italianate terrace as part of the set, and surrounding the audience with actors entering and exiting from all sides and through the centre aisle of the natural amphitheatre. The trees themselves became part of the cast, as in the 1982 *Macbeth*, when the witches seemed to emerge from the trunk of one of them. With her emphasis on multicultural casting, Packer created a vision of the future in *Romeo and Juliet*, *Twelfth Night* and *Comedy of Errors* while probing present and past in *The Tempest*.

Frank Rich wrote that Shakespeare & Company's production of *Twelfth Night* conjured for him the words of O'Neill's James Tyrone when he tells his son, 'I would have acted in any of [Shakespeare's] plays for nothing, for the joy of being alive in his great poetry' (1981). This sentiment captures the youthful energy of that first decade when company members had more poetry than money to sustain them, perhaps feeling most alive when their voices reached out to the audience as the sun set on the sloping lawn.

2

And we'll look, not at visions, but at realities[1]

By 1988 the company was known for speaking Shakespearean verse so clearly that, as one reviewer wrote, 'it sounds as lucid and familiar as the morning radio news, even to the uninitiated' (Brantley 2008: B11). Under Packer's artistic leadership the company continued expand and create innovative productions and performance spaces. Each theatre space invited different modes of actor–audience interaction, from the intimate indoor Salon theatre in the main house, where the company produced original plays adapted from Wharton's short stories, to the Stables theatre, inside Wharton's former horse stable, to the outdoor mainstage. In 1988 geometer Rachel Fletcher redesigned the outdoor mainstage to align it on the property according to Renaissance and classical architectural concepts of harmony.

In this chapter, I examine three of Packer's critically acclaimed, innovative productions from her second decade: *As You Like It* was produced with a large cast on the outdoor mainstage in her grand mise en scène style while *Julius Caesar* and *Measure for Measure* were minimalist productions in her new bare bard style, developed for the intimate 108 seat indoor Stables theatre. These productions, modelled after the touring companies of Shakespeare's day, utilized casts of six to eight actors playing multiple roles on minimalist sets. For

Julius Caesar Packer's staging was inspired by play's statue motif while her *Measure for Measure* used multiple casting to emphasize how the play blurs the lines of high and low characters embodying Renaissance dichotomies of angel and devil, virtue and vice. I discuss how Packer's methods encourage actors to reveal themselves through the language of their characters, inviting them to inhabit the language as experience with the goal of creating productions that are not only entertaining, but illuminating and provocative as well. I frame these case studies with a survey of all the productions she directed in her second decade. These productions show her continuing commitment to engaging her audience with multicultural casting, now using two different styles of staging Shakespeare's plays.

To the centre and out: *As You Like It*, 1988

Tina Packer opened her company's second decade at The Mount with *As You Like It* featuring Karen Allen who by 1988 was a film star. Her Marion, opposite Harrison Ford's Indiana Jones in the 1981 blockbuster hit *Raiders of the Lost Ark*, cemented her gritty, warm, sweetheart status: 'Allen projects empathy, accessibility and sweet intelligence ... This is more than a (very) pretty face: this is someone you can talk to, someone who'll *understand* ... ' (Turan 1985: 34). With her approachable charm, Allen was ideal for the role of Rosalind in Shakespeare's celebration of the pastoral world, in an open-air setting that was ideal for the play: 'The natural forest amplified and caressed their voices. In fact, it electrified and deepened every cranny of the production. Feet crunched needle rugs; running actors cast animated shadows on trees and paths; words diminished, intensified, rebounded. One almost heard thoughts in bark, tongues in brooks, sermons in stones' (Gehman 1989: 20). Meanwhile 'Bruce Odland's score add[ed] distant liquid chitterings and horn calls as well as violin and guitar bowings and pluckings' while 'As night falls, lighting designer Arden Fingerhut takes over with a lovely feeling for the natural setting' (Taylor 1988: 10).

Allen's performance was well-received. One critic opined: 'Hers is not an incandescent Vanessa Redgrave Rosalind. But the vigorous commitment she brings to the role grows ... as the production progresses ... And Rosalind's famous epilogue ... is particularly effective as delivered by Allen with unaffected high spirits' (Taylor 1988: 10). Another wrote that she was 'shimmering and radiant' and that 'this is a Rosalind to be reckoned with' (Borak 1988: D1).

The vocal qualities and physical energy of the cast were the product of an intense, dynamic and playful rehearsal process. As Jonathan Epstein recalled, 'The rehearsals were challenging and joyful ... we were working at a deep level on every aspect of the play's language: the sound, the meaning, the implications. We were very big voiced: the language of the cast had a musicality and a size that effortlessly filled the outdoor space without microphones' (2022b).

In *As You Like It*, as Packer observes, the heroine's journey is not only physical and psychological, sexual and spiritual, 'it is also a journey of independence ... women find new selves in their disguise, facets of themselves they then use to forward the story and their relationships' (2016: 178–9). Packer writes that like the rose that gives Rosalind her name, 'The layers of these love plays are always curled inside one another, going to a center and connecting to the outside world' (2016: 188).

Packer's description of the rose, with its layers curling towards the centre and opening out to connect with the world, is an apt description of how she guided her cast on their individual and collective journeys through the world of the play in the rehearsal process. Her directing unfolded in layers around the play's language, building the world of the production from the words of the text. Through this process the actors delved into their psyches, emotions and experiences, so that the vibrations of this energy would connect and resonate with the audience.

Packer had seven weeks of rehearsal time as well as a strong cast comprised of long-standing company members and some, like Allen, who were new to the company. The first layer of rehearsal took the cast through a week of *dropping in*. The next layer guided the actors through several weeks that deepened the discoveries of *dropping in* with daily rotations through scene rehearsal and staging with Packer, voice with Kristin Linklater, dance and movement with Susan Dibble, music with Bruce Odland, and *First Folio* text with Neil Freeman. Throughout the process the cast circled up in the rehearsal space at the beginning and end of each day. As a complement to the intensity of *dropping in* and the in-depth work on staging, voice and text, Packer created a playful exercise for the entire cast in order to reinforce the cast's sense of community while inviting them to forge an embodied connection to the play's world by tapping into their individual and collective creative energy.

Telling tales of Sir Rowland de Boys

The exercise took its cue from Duke Frederick and his comrades in the forest of Arden, who pass the time by telling stories. During the third week of rehearsal, Packer asked her cast to circle up and tell stories about Sir Rowland de Boys, who haunts the play and whom she sees as a central figure. He is the father of Oliver, Orlando and the plays' other 'Jaques', who shows up at the end to announce Duke Frederick's conversion. The name Rowland de Boys evokes the tales of Charlemagne and his brave knight, Sir Roland who was celebrated by French troubadours in the long-ago age of chivalry. For the production, Packer had his 'horn call sounded in the distance whenever the name Sir Rowland de Boys was uttered or honour was invoked' (Epstein 2022b).

Her instructions to the cast were for each actor to be in character for the exercise and to imagine and then share with the group how their character was connected to Sir Rowland de Boys. For example, maybe they knew him first hand, or merely heard about him. Perhaps they knew stories no one else knew. The activity, improvisatory in nature, began and continued on impulse in order to allow the cast's creative energy to flow freely. The group awaited the first person to speak and the activity continued as the next person spoke on impulse to tell their tale. The exercise elicited and developed the imaginative energy of the actors, simultaneously drawing them deeper into the world of the play while bringing them closer as a community as they moved through the rehearsal process towards opening night, where that energy was present in their performances.

Packer is known as a director who asks questions to guide her actors rather than one who tells them what to do. Even so, she adapts to the needs of each actor as necessary. On the way to opening night Packer often takes time to work with actors individually. In what follows, three of the actors she worked with for *As You Like It* share their experiences of working with her. Their journeys show how Packer adapted her approach based upon her knowledge of the actor's capabilities and the needs of the production. She wants her actors to work as deeply as possible but does not push them. It is for them to push themselves when they are ready. Each of these actors had a different relationship with Packer, who is a keen observer. In Midori Nakamura, Packer knew she had a talented actor with exceptional gymnastic strength and skill. Jonathan Epstein, who was new to the company, was experienced, intelligent and strong-willed, while Timothy Douglas, she had recently learned, had a background in musical theatre. She knew that he was gay, and she wanted him to make that part of his character. Each actor's journey required a different approach on Packer's part. She expanded Midori Nakamura's comic repertoire through physical comedy; she sparred with Jonathan

Epstein; and she gave Timothy Douglas the encouragement and freedom to discover himself in his multiple roles, particularly that of Le Beau.

Three actor's journeys

Midori Nakamura: Celia as clown

Packer is well-versed in standard comic form and pratfalls and uses them when she knows the actor is capable of executing them. In this instance, she guided Nakamura's creative physical energy into a non-daily modality using standard comic forms. Midori Nakamura was new to the company, having attended the 1988 winter training intensive at the company where she met Karen Allen, who was participating in the training at the invitation of Kristin Linklater, with whom Allen had been doing voice work. At the conclusion of the workshop, Packer asked Allen if she would like to play Rosalind and if she had anyone in mind for Celia. Allen and Nakamura developed excellent rapport during the intensive, so she suggested Nakamura. Packer was impressed with Nakamura's talent and saw in her someone who could ably handle physical comedy. Allen and Nakamura had a delightful sense of game in their relationship and journey in the play, helped along by Packer's direction. As Nakamura recalled, 'Tina used all the classic gags, the physical gags, and pratfalls. I love them. I found it to be a lot of fun. She gave me a lot of that direction, which I liked. I thought it would open up things that I wouldn't necessarily have done or thought or considered. And I just went for it' (2022). In Nakamura, Packer had an actor who was capable of taking physical comedy to the edge.

For example, when Rosalind, Touchstone and Celia enter at the top of scene 2.4, Celia is exhausted from wandering in the forest: 'Tina told me to say my line in a perfectly normal fashion … And then just fall over' (2022). Nakamura recalled:

Tina wanted me to be totally straight, falling over very slowly, and then, boom. There were technical aspects to it that I recognized. For example, I understood the rhythm of falling over that she described, and that my body had to stay stiff, which the body does not do if you lose consciousness. But my body had to stay stiff and then I almost had to bounce at the bottom. I could do all of that because I had come out of intense physical training ... I couldn't see it of course, but it always got a huge laugh. Celia is very self-dramatizing. Hence the pratfall and hence you better carry me because I'm just so out. I'm done. (2022)

This moment marked a change in the dynamic between Celia and Rosalind, as Nakamura explained:

There's shifting that goes back and forth in their relationship. On some level, it's very much a game: 'let's play this, we've never played that, won't that be fun? Hey, let's get dressed like men. Let's go into the forest. Let's find my uncle'. Rosalind follows Celia to the forest, but the way Tina staged it was that, by the time we're actually in the forest, Rosalind is forging ahead, and in her element, and suddenly, I'm [Celia] exhausted. (2022)

Nakamura highlighted another moment in which Packer gave her direction to help her find the humour in the scene. In scene 3.2 Rosalind, Celia and Le Beau discover Orland's poems posted on trees. Celia finds the longest poem and reads it aloud to everyone's delight, especially Rosalind's. Packer helped Nakamura inhabit the physical humour of reading the poem. As Nakamura recalled, 'Tina said the rhythm of the poem has to be in your feet. And then it will work. And then have fun playing with that rhythm and finding the rhythm in your feet' (2022). Packer's casting of Nakamura in the role of Celia was astute. Her Celia was noted by reviewers for her wonderfully comic performance, which brought new dimensions to the Celia–Rosalind dynamic: 'Midori Nakamura's lively, anti-man

Celia provides a wickedly youthful foil to Allen's Rosalind – until this Celia falls with an open-mouthed thud for the reformed Oliver' (Taylor 1988: 10). As Nakamura explained, through the rehearsal process she realized, 'Celia is an excellent observer, but has had little experience with romantic involvement. She's full of judgment, but not insight. The way she has to fall in love is not through a lot of pondering or self-aware consideration. This what she knows. And then, the game changes' (2022). Reviewers uniformly found Nakamura's Celia 'outrageously funny', as one of them put it. (Gordon 1988: 41).

Packer's direction elicited a wonderfully comic Celia from Midori Nakamura, while her collaboration with Jonathan Epstein developed a unique interpretation that resulted in a Jaques for the ages.

Jonathan Epstein: Extreme Jaques

In this next example Packer worked with Jonathan Epstein, playing against his energy in a way that mirrored the relationship between Jaques and Duke Senior. Packer and Epstein are both superb actors, highly intelligent and strong-willed. Packer met Epstein in 1987 when he auditioned for and was cast by Packer for the Boston Shakespeare Company's *Rat and the Skull* and *Double Cross,* which opened in the winter of 1987. The two collaborated well, and Epstein took the winter training intensive at the company in 1988. Epstein recalled that although he was an experienced actor, skilled at individualized characterization, he 'was about to run out of roles I was good enough to play … I tended to play intelligent villains of one kind or another, and there wasn't a lot of spontaneity in my acting. I didn't do much comedy' (2021). Subsequently, 'as a result of the '88 workshop and working with Tina on *As You Like It*, a whole range of roles became accessible to me because I opened up and became less stiff, more capable of using everything I have to bring to a role' (2021).

Epstein's work with Packer on the role of Jaques, in the 1988 production of *As You Like It* resulted in an original interpretation that was an astonishing success. In Packer's group exercise, 'Telling Tales of Sir Rowland de Boys', Epstein's Jaques spoke of his close friendship with Sir Rowland and Duke Senior, which, as Epstein explained, was cemented by their having 'gone to war together. Rowland returned from the war to his estate. The duke had returned because his father died. I (Jaques) stayed abroad, living in Turkey and the Near east' (2022a). For Epstein, Jaques's opening line, 'More More, I prithee More! (2.5.9), was the key to his character: 'Staying in the Near East after the wars wasn't just happenstance, it was an expression of Jaques' lifelong voracious appetite for larger and larger experiences, which is typified by his first line' (2022a). Epstein took his cue for Jaques's friendship with Duke Senior from the duke's curiosity over Jaques's whereabouts in scene 2.1. After the group exercise, Packer and Epstein agreed that from this perspective when Jaques makes his first entrance in the play, appearing in the forest, he is a war veteran armed with tales of adventure. Packer and Epstein agreed as well that there was a danger that Jaques might become too sympathetic, as onstage and offstage audiences listened, rapt, to his monologues. There is indeed a tendency in productions of *As You Like It* for Jaques to slow down the unfolding action with his philosophical musings. In many productions this is intentional as well as successful, particularly with a well-known actor in the role. Yet Packer wanted her *As You Like It* to be playful, light on its feet and fast-paced. Epstein's unique characterization resulted from Packer's concern that the role might unbalance the play's energy if the character were too sympathetic and poetic. As Epstein recalled, 'The risk is that Jaques become contemplative or ruminative – not because that wouldn't make sense with the language – most of it – but because it can kill the momentum of the play. So in a sense we were working backwards from a desired result – driving energy [in the character] – to find a cause' (2022a). This was a conundrum because of Packer's emphasis on working deeply. Epstein needed resistance to work against so that what appeared to be contemplative lines could be played instead with a genuine sense of urgency. Epstein looked to the text, finding clues to Jaques's malady when the duke chides him: 'For thou thyself hast been a libertine, / As sensual as the brutish sting itself, / And all those embossed sores and headed evils / That thou with license of free foot hast caught / Wouldst thou disgorge into the general world' (2.7.64–69). While acknowledging that this passage is, perhaps, meant metaphorically, Packer and Epstein decided to take it literally:

> The driving energy that Tina wanted from Jaques only made sense if he had to drive through some resistance to being heard. If the pages think of Jaques as a sweet old guy with valuable insights there's no resistance and no need to drive the play. However, if Jaques is clearly diseased, unwashed and batshit crazy, then no-one wants to hear him and he needs to find ways of insisting on being heard. (2022a)

Epstein researched 'ailments of the mind in the 16th century' and soon discovered that syphilis aligned with Jaques's arc in the play:

> Syphilis, in its tertiary stage can result in megalomania, violent mood swings and osteomyelitis. The treatment was sweating with mercury vapor which results in manic volubility. In the forest, the syphilis would persist but there would be no access to mercury, so the volubility would abate, which is in fact what happens to Jaques – still crazy but the big word-avalanches don't happen anymore after Seven Ages. (2022a)

Epstein created a look for Jaques that corresponded with his malady: 'Your bones start collapsing. So typically, your cheekbones and nose will actually fall apart. I built for myself a kind of a prosthetic that went over my nose with a big black piece of fabric in it. It looked like there was a hole in my nose. And then I had a silver nose piece that went over that' (2022a).

Reviewers saw contemporary relevance in Epstein's portrayal of Jaques:

> Jaques appears to be rotting away physically, presumably from a venereal disease. He wears a silver nose which, when removed briefly, reveals black, deteriorating flesh beneath. The 'codpiece' Jaques wears on his nose echoes the blatant, scarlet codpiece the clown Touchstone flaunts. And both underscore the production's acknowledgement of Shakespeare's bawdiness ... as well as the vivid anti-romantic side of the comedy's romanticism. Love and sexual attraction can exult. But they can also kill. Shakespeare's play is all too pertinent in this AIDS era. (Taylor 1988: 10)

At the same time, Packer succeeded in keeping the play balanced: 'Not that the production is at all heavy-handed in this respect. It balances the romantic and anti-romantic very well, and the play's bucolic, pastoral charm is attractively served' (Taylor 1988: 10).

The dynamic between Packer and Epstein had a sense of sparring not unlike that between Duke Senior and Jaques. During one rehearsal, Epstein recalled:

> I did the Seven Ages of Man speech and she didn't know quite what to say about it. So she said, 'Well, just do it again, but do everything different, every word' ... I did it six or seven times in a row, not doing anything the same. And by the time we were done with it that particular day, we really had a good sense of where we wanted to go with that speech. (2022a)

Everything was humming along until they timed the first dress rehearsal. The play was running around three hours and forty minutes. They had to cut time, so Packer asked the cast to do a speed through:

> I'm not born yesterday. I know what happens in speed throughs: everybody goes pretty fast, and then the director says, 'Okay, do it like that'. So, I went unbelievably fast. I went faster than anybody can go. I went insanely fast, figuring I've got this outsmarted – Tina will say, 'Everybody, do it like that, except Jonny. You can slow down a little bit'. But of course, she didn't say that. She said, 'Everybody do it like that'. I said, 'Well, even me?' She says, 'Yes'. I was furious. I felt I'd wasted a lot of rehearsal time. I thought, 'well, there's my Jaques – gone. All my beautiful melancholy'. (Epstein 2022a)

Once the production opened, the sharp-witted theatre reviewer, Carolyn Clay wrote: 'Jonathan Epstein's unusually vigorous Jaques does not so much wallow in his melancholy as jump into its saddle and ride' (Clay 1988: 9). Epstein read the review and thought, 'oh yeah, that is what I'm doing. That sounds cool' (2022a).

While Packer's collaborative combat with Epstein challenged him to outdo himself in the role of Jaques, she was the catalyst for Timothy Douglas's difficult yet ultimately exhilarating unveiling in the role of LeBeau.

Timothy Douglas: Working from where you are

One of Packer's central tenets is that connecting with the audience on a deep level requires actors to reveal themselves through their characters by allowing all the dimensions of emotion to be present in their performances. *Dropping in* helps the actors take ownership over Shakespeare's words through the creative process of exploring the emotions and memories that surface with each word of the text. It also requires letting go of inhibitions that cause tension throughout the body and prevent the voice from resonating as fully as possible. This means accepting who you are as well as whatever emotional or psychological struggles you are having. Instead of trying to ignore or suppress them, actors are encouraged to acknowledge them and allow them to be present. It is Packer's contention that:

> Once the actor stands in front of the audience, all the things we hope people will recognise in us will be seen, but all the things we want to hide will remain hidden, and those hopes and fears block the actors' ability to be completely vulnerable in front of the audience – which is of course what the greatest actors are able to do. (2023b)

The following experience, related by Timothy Douglas, demonstrates what this means. Douglas was a company member with a background in musical theatre. Packer cast him in three roles: Amiens, Le Beau and Hymen. Douglas, who is gay, recalled that until playing Le Beau in this production, 'I'd never played flamboyantly gay on stage' (2022). Douglas found it 'confronting … Tina really encouraged a high level of flamboyance in my portrayal of the role, which became increasingly complicated for me' (2022). Packer recalled that Douglas 'Had everything within him to play the roles, especially Le Beau, and my job was to help him do that by encouraging him to reveal those aspects of himself' (2023b). During the rehearsal process, the complexity of what was being asked of Douglas came into focus:

> It had to do with the world I was coming from as a young Black man, the deeply intricate homophobic aspects within it, and how I was socialized by it: openly gay was to be made fun of and was to be shamed. In the objective, as an actor, I could intuit the possibility of embodying the character as a whole being, which is why I struggled to understand why it was so challenging for me. It should have just been fun. It was fun and then it became increasingly burdensome … It was a point in my developmental process as an actor when I was starting to absorb the foundational principle of 'going from where you are', which I fully came to appreciate during my tenure at Shakespeare & Company, so I understood that it was essential that I allow my complicated feelings to be part of the journey – in particular within the heightened flamboyance of that performance. (2022)

When Douglas acknowledged his complicated feelings, let go, and revealed himself in the role, his performance shifted:

> That's exactly when I started getting very succinct feedback from Tina, feedback I could work with on a process as opposed to a performance level. That carriage had arrived. Even from Karen Allen, who acknowledged the difference in our scenes where now I was fully there, and with an edge, with a facility to impact that I didn't even know that I possessed. The open gayness ended up reading as 'me' being open and out, while the role's outward manifestation of flamboyant feminineness had all to do with the inflated size of Le Beau's belief in his perception of what power feels and looks like. (2022)

As Douglas explained, he was 'sending up the character, while at the same time taking the character seriously. That seriousness grounded me enough to be able to work through the feelings of shame that were coming up for me' (2022). In this way, he 'claimed the power of being in the know, even if it was just with those two women – Rosalind and Celia' (2022). It translated into the wrestling scene where 'Le Beau had very big presence – both in portrayal and augmented direction from Tina … It was made even clearer to me by the response of the onstage crowd, along with the audience's, all of whom were taking their cue from Le Beau' (2022).

Packer saw in Douglas's Le Beau a comic version of Wittrock's Orlando. For the wrestling match she heightened that dynamic by having Le Beau lead both the onstage and theatre audiences in their cheers for Orlando. Douglas could feel them responding to him:

> I experienced how organically my presence unfolded once I fully stepped into the role, bringing into play all these aspects of myself, and of the character. It included openly flirting with Orlando (Peter Wittrock) while giving him the news that someone likes him and Karen Allen's Rosalind and Midori Nakamura's Celia picking up on that. I was part of a trio with them, which was gratifying for both my character and for me as an actor. (2022)

Douglas's Le Beau was costumed in black balloon pants over yellow tights with horizontal black stripes sewn into them, with a matching vest and a hat garnished with a big yellow and black bow: 'The cast called me the bumblebee and somehow Kiki Smith (the designer) found platform shoes in my size ... I'm running around that outdoor playing space in these platform shoes, navigating brilliantly, as only a drag queen could' (2022). One reviewer wrote that Douglas gave 'a delicious performance as Le Beau, a foppish courtier, that contrasts nicely with his amiable Amiens' (Borak 1988: B 10). Packer recalled how deeply the trio of them cared for each other: 'Le Beau really liked Celia and Rosalind, they had a wonderful rapport, even though beneath the scene's comedy they were all in a dangerous position at the wrestling match because of Orlando's need to fight for his inheritance as the son of Sir Rowland' (2023a). She recalled the excitement and energy of the scene, particularly when 'Le Beau began to lead the audience in chants for Orlando to win the match' (2023a).

As these three journeys show, Packer adapts her directing based upon her actors' individual needs. In this way she anchors the cast while guiding their work as a collaborative process, creating both the structure and the space for them to breathe, play and discover, much in the way the characters of *As You Like It* find new selves in the forest.

The next year Packer repeated the formula of bringing in a star actor for the leading role supported by her talented and well-trained ensemble. She invited André Gregory and his daughter Marina to play Prospero and Miranda for her 1989 mainstage production of *The Tempest*. Keanu Reeves played Trinculo while Rocco Sisto, who is white, played Caliban, in a performance described as 'electric' (Gehman 1989: 15). Kenny Ransom, who is Black, played Ferdinand. Her 1989 *Tempest* thus reversed the casting of her 1980 *Tempest* where Caliban was Black and Ferdinand was white. Midori Nakamura was a luminous, courageous 'otherwordly' Ariel, with 'the power to spin both air and fire' (Kelly 1989: 55). The critical consensus was that the production was 'simply wonderful ... [d]espite the Gregorys' (Kelly 1989: 55). In 1990 Packer restaged *As You Like It* as a cost-saving measure, this time with Karen MacDonald as Rosalind. Many loved her Rosalind, others felt it was too soon to present the play again, particularly after the excitement of seeing Karen Allen on stage.

Early in 1992, Packer solidified her return to acting, accepting the role of Shirley Valentine for a six week run at the Charles Playhouse in Boston. Her performance received wide acclaim. As one reviewer wrote, 'her Shirley reaches out to us as friends, as confidantes, as accomplices', and concluded that Packer is a 'great actress who can evoke the tears in humor and the laughter in heartbreak' (Friedman 1992: 51). At the time, Packer, related, 'The invitation to play the role coincided with me trying to get in touch with who I am as a person ... as opposed to this machine who tried to run two theater companies' (Fanger 1992: S 19).[2]

Moving statues: *Julius Caesar*, 1992–3

In 1992 Packer inaugurated a new style of staging Shakespeare at The Mount. This proved to be an important development in her directorial work. She launched her bare bard *Julius Caesar* for matinee performances in Edith Wharton's former horse stables, thereby adapting an existing structure to serve as an indoor theatre. The intimate, rough-hewn space proved to be an ideal match for her elegantly spare production that explored the tangled passions and politics of Rome in 44 BCE. Her 1992 matinee was a thrilling success, so Packer remounted it the next summer season in 1993 as an evening prime-time show to critical acclaim. The production stands out as among the most inspired in her oeuvre. This case study follows its development through the discoveries made in the 1992 rehearsal process to its 1993 critical reception.[3]

Packer's bare bards are the opposite of her grand mise en scène productions, employing six to eight actors playing all the roles instead of casts of forty or more on the outdoor stage. The design elements are minimal and innovative. Tod Randolph, who played five different roles in *Julius Caesar*, recalled, 'Tina wanted us to turn our bodies into the set, as it were' (2021). Packer took her cue from the way Shakespeare transposes the play's characters into their statues, as in Calpurnia's dream of Caesar's 'statue spouting blood' (2.2.85). The play interrogates the permeable boundary between character and statue in the Roman ethos with this potent trope manifesting the characters' awareness of their simultaneous place on the Renaissance stage and the stage of history. Packer used this idea for the theme, design and movement of the production.

The show opened with the seven actors introducing themselves and their roles before taking up the postures of Roman statues on their respective plinths positioned on the shallow stage. Kevin Kelly of *The Boston Globe* saw contemporary resonances in their costumes: 'John Pennoyer's costumes – reversible cloaks worn over dark shirts and britches – have a style suggesting the murderous reach of political ambition stretching from the Roman Senate to the White House' (1993: 67). Pennoyer made the cloaks reversible, with one side buff (the Caesar party), and the other cream (the Brutus party) in order to facilitate seamless, rapid changes of character. When the actors needed to change character to the opposite side, they swirled around and reversed the cloak (Epstein 2022a). This rapid physical switching of characters and political affiliations viscerally manifested the tumultuous passions underpinning the political dynamics in the play. The energy created by this movement coupled with the actor's resonant voices in the intimate space drew the audience into the play's action. The actors would come alive, step off their plinths, play their scene or collectively create tableaux that physicalized the images in the text, then return to their statue postures on the plinths. The result was a rhythmic pattern, emphasized by a percussive kettle drum, punctuating the intimate two person scenes and more populated senate and battle scenes with moments of swirling movement. Often, within a scene when one actor was speaking, others performed the imagery of the text. These moments were created in rehearsal with long-time company movement specialist and choreographer Susan Dibble. As Jonathan Epstein, who played Brutus, recalled,

> For the first week and a half or so, which is when we created the first half of the play, we basically sculpted. Susan would have some of her magical music playing, and prompt us to create tableaux vivant or deep relief sculptures of all the events, as if we were the crown of the Parthenon, the Elgin marbles. So as one person would be talking, others behind them would be sculpting the event. (2022a)

For example, 'when Casca (James Robert Daniels) said "A common slave – you know him well by sight – / Held up his left hand, which did flame and burn / Like twenty torches joined" (1.3.15–17), there was Tod with her hand on fire and everyone else making flames' (Epstein 2022a). On the line 'dogs of war' (3.1.276), the cast became barking dogs (Epstein 2022a). Kevin Kelly of *The Boston Globe* found the staging vivid: 'When Shakespeare passingly mentions a "bird of night," Randolph is "flown" into the scene on an actor's shoulder, her arms fluttering. When the conspirators gather together, they share the physical camaraderie of a closed men's club, then stand still as a frieze' (1993: 67). Ben Brantley of *The New York Times* praised Dibble's work: 'The seven-member ensemble, playing multiple roles, acts out the spoken descriptions of dreams, memories and portents, which abound in this work, with statuesque poses that recall the choreography of Martha Graham. The effect is to provide, disturbingly, fixed iconographic equivalents to the specters that dominate a public's collective imagination in a time of political turmoil' (1993: C2). Susan Dibble credited the actors: '[They] were the creators; they made my ideas and suggestions about form come alive. It is that experience with the actors that captures the most important thing about working on a play with Tina – exploration and finding the story in the body – three dimensionality at its core' (2022b).

The rehearsal period for the 1992 matinee production was short. The cast, all established company members who had worked together before, began rehearsals while the company was teaching a workshop at Simon's Rock in Great Barrington, Massachusetts. Epstein noted that everyone in the cast knew all the lines in the play. With most of the cast playing multiple roles, many were in every scene. Packer's *dropping in* requires everyone who is in the scene to be present, whether or not they have lines. The cast rehearsed in the mornings and taught in the workshop in the afternoons. Packer held check-ins at the beginning and end of each rehearsal day. For *Julius Caesar* Packer was interested in the play's mob violence and asked the cast to read Bill Buford's *Among the Thugs: The Experience, and Seduction, of Crowd Violence* about football hooliganism in the United Kingdom. The goal, as Epstein explained, 'was for us to get a sense of the mob mentality, the extreme violence that results in the death of Cinna the Poet' (2022a). Packer asked cast members to research their characters by reading Plutarch and other sources. Each actor then presented a report to the group about what they discovered. The research changed Epstein's mind about the idea of honour: 'I would say that for me, the idea of honor as a positive virtue rather than an absence of shame – that something is honorable in itself – really came out of this production' (2022a). He realized that 'Brutus makes mistakes, not because he is imperceptive or weak, but because he refuses to think ill of people … He insists on having honorable thoughts about other people, because he wants to have honorable thoughts about himself' (2022a). As Epstein sees it, 'Everybody loved Brutus, and in a way, Brutus loved everybody. His love is his most powerful attribute' (2022a). Epstein reached this understanding of his character through *dropping in* with Packer as well as through the research and discussion that Packer encouraged. These laid the groundwork for further discovery during scene rehearsal.

Epstein (Brutus) and Coleman (Cassius) were often given the freedom to rehearse on their own because they were two of Packer's most experienced actors and the rehearsals were taking place while the company was also leading a workshop that required Packer's presence.

As they rehearsed the play that first year in early spring, Coleman recalled, 'what we kept discovering until we couldn't deny it anymore was that this play is a love story of these iconic individuals. They are deeply flawed, but they deeply love each other – Cassius and Brutus, Caesar and Brutus, Calpurnia and Caesar, Portia and Brutus – it's a love story' (2022a). This discovery manifests itself, in particular, in the relationship between Cassius and Brutus. Coleman explained, 'You can hear it in the tent scene, the constant use of personal pronouns. It's you, you, me, myself, you, me, I, you – and what starts coming up is that this is a fight between two people who deeply love each other and are hurt. It's a love scene. It's very personal. It's not about politics, it's about, "you love me not" and "I do not like your faults"' (2022a).

Coleman described Packer's approach to directing as generous: 'She would give us a lot of room. She wasn't a fastidious director. She would excite you with an idea, and then let you play. Then she would respond to what you were doing' (2022a). After they worked on the tent scene, they showed it to Packer, as Epstein recalled:

> We did it, and she said, 'That was great.' And we did it again, and that was great. We never staged the tent scene. For two years, Kevin and I played the tent scene, he, pulling his sword, me throwing him his sword, and never staged it. We had so much confidence in each other. I knew what he needed to get out of the tent scene. He knew what I needed to get out of the tent scene. We both knew what Tina needed to get out of the tent scene. And if one thing got shifted, something else got shifted to accommodate it. I mean, really, I don't think I've ever had that relationship with a scene partner before or since. (2022a)

The production demonstrates the success of Packer's approach with an ensemble of experienced actors who know each other well from working together. She inspired her cast and artistic crew with an exciting idea that stimulated and focussed their energy. Then she let them play. Perhaps the most telling moment for the playfulness, energy and focus that permeated the entire process, from the first rehearsal to the matinee performances to the 1993 remounting, was the moment when Cassius, played by Kevin Coleman, told Brutus (Epstein) of his devotion to Caesar (1.2.102–8). Epstein recalled: On the line, 'Accoutred as I was I plungèd in', Coleman 'took a flying leap forward towards the audience and James Rice and I, knowing Kevin, were there and caught him. We hadn't talked about it. He jumped; we caught him. That was the degree of trust and excitement that pervaded. It was freezing cold, early in spring – we were being magic and we knew it' (Epstein 2022a).

Over the course of the rehearsal process, at the beginning and end of the day, the cast circled up to share discoveries. The discovery between Jonathan Epstein and Kevin Coleman was a direct result of how Packer directs, even though she wasn't always in the room when they were working. These were two accomplished actors that Packer knew well, and she left them alone to play until it was time for her to be their audience, and make suggestions by asking questions rather than telling them what to do. Another pair of actors may have made a different discovery. While the text certainly suggests love between Cassius and Brutus, it doesn't define the particular quality of that love. Because the actors themselves discovered it, they owned its energy, with all the bewilderment, initial resistance and excitement of the discovery, in all its varied shades of feeling, from surprise to surrender, all of which remained in their bodies and psyches for the performance. The success of this production exemplifies Packer's conviction that transformative theatre depends upon giving actors the guidance and space to discover and create out of their unique experiences and psyches. In doing so, they delve into the underlying emotional tapestry of their scene in a particular moment with a specific cast. Packer believes that when actors inhabit the difficult emotions created and elicited through their engagement with the text, their experience resonates with the audience on a visceral level. The farewell scene between Cassius and Brutus exemplified this dynamic. It was performed downstage, close to the audience. The combination of the 'austerity of it and the degree to which Coleman and Epstein were locked in with each other' had the audience sobbing nearly every performance (Epstein 2022). Epstein's performance, open and vulnerable, drew them in to Brutus's tragedy: 'Packer is wonderful in her direction of Jonathan Epstein as Brutus, who weeps uncontrollably when the awful cost of his vengeance-for-a greater-good becomes known to him. Epstein's performance is bitterly then sorrowfully majestic' (Kelly 1993: 67). The emotional resonance of the performances was accentuated by the steel drum as the cast shifted from moments of swirling movement and emotional intensity to stillness.

The multiple casting deployed clever staging that intensified the tragic dimensions of the production, particularly with Tod Randolph, who played Brutus's servant, Lucius, as well as Calpurnia and Portia. Both wives endeavour to be heard by their husbands. Caesar ultimately dismisses Calpurnia's dream: 'How foolish do your fears seem now, Calpurnia / I am ashamed I did yield to them' (2.2.105–6). Brutus puts off sharing with Portia what preoccupies him: 'Portia, go in a while, / And by and by thy bosom shall partake / The secrets of my heart' (2.1.303–305). Packer emphasized the simultaneous importance and impotence of the matrons of Rome by locating Tod Randolph upstage as a statue of the female spirit of Rome when she wasn't playing her other roles. This statuesque feminine presence hovered in the air after first Epstein's Brutus refused to take Portia into his confidence and subsequently when Malcolm Ingram's Caesar dismissed Calpurnia's premonition when Decius shamed him (2.2.96–99). As Katharine Eisaman Maus writes, 'The "feminine intuition" that both women possess in abundance has no practical effect' (2008: 1553). Neither 'Caesar nor Brutus can risk being seen to be influenced by a mere wife' (2008: 1553). Maus sees the 'two successive accounts' of Portia's suicide as Shakespeare's 'skill in delineating character': in private, Brutus shares his loss and grief with Cassius (2008: 1553). Later when he is with his army, and Messala tells him that Portia died in 'strange manner' (4.2.241), Brutus 'affects a studied indifference ... for true "Romans" are willing to incur huge emotional costs for what they imagine is the greater good' (2008: 1553). Packer deepened the tragic irony of the Roman ethos of honour in the staging of Brutus's death. She cut the role of Strato, so Brutus's servant, Lucius, held the sword for Brutus in his death scene. Packer staged the scene so that Randolph, who played both Lucius and Portia, held the sword as Lucius, at Brutus's order, 'Hold then my sword, and turn away thy face / While I do run upon it' (5.5.47–48). Then, as Brutus spoke his dying words, 'Caesar now be still / I killed not thee with half so good a will' (5.5.50–51), Randolph let her hair down, instantaneously becoming Portia. Brutus died looking at his wife. The moment captured the poignancy and incomprehension of Brutus's tragedy:

> Brutus appears to us in several guises: as a public figure, a husband, a master of servants, a military leader. Thus he experiences painfully in his own person the value conflicts that are dispersed among various antagonists. How is Brutus – and how are we – to reconcile his tender regard for his wife and servant with his willingness to commit political murder? (Maus 2008: 1551)

For Ben Brantley, Epstein's interpretation of Brutus was reminiscent of Hamlet: 'Mr. Epstein [is] a sonorously melancholy Brutus, played as a direct ancestor to Hamlet' (1993). Brantley also singled out Malcolm Ingram, who 'splendidly conveys both the glamour and fatuity of Caesar' (1993: C2). Kevin Kelly observed that 'what Tina Packer has accomplished is a minimalist "Julius Caesar" with all the major philosophic sonorities. Seven actors announce themselves by name, specify the characters they play, then, hiding their real identities under cloaks, step into a bare, garishly lighted room where – against the occasional shake of copper thunder – they provide something close to a sweep of greatness' (1993: 67).

The production was not only a critical success, it was a success for those in the ensemble: 'We had a lot of trouble with money at that time, but we knew we were giving a fabulous show. I don't think I've ever left the theater feeling lighter and more in a sense connected with what it is' (Epstein 2022a).

The same year Packer directed a 'spectacular' (Brown 1994: 12) mainstage production of *A Midsummer Night's Dream*, doubling the roles of Hippolyta and Titania, Theseus and Oberon, à la Peter Brook. She opened the play with a battle scene between the Amazons and the Greeks that ended in single combat between Corinna May's white Hippolyta and Kenny Ransom's Black Theseus: 'Both gorgeously lithe actors [they] fought desperately, with groans and snarls punctuated by thuds. Hippolyta threw Theseus twice, believably. Theseus briefly mounted Hippolyta, but she threw him off' (Brown 1994: 11). The fight ended as their physicality grew amatory and segued into the play's opening lines. The production was 'very physical' while also poetic: 'Ransom gave [his] words a thrilling lilt' (Brown 1994: 11).

In 1995, Packer's *Much Ado about Nothing* was listed among 'The Best of 1995' in *The Boston Globe*: (1995: 35). One reviewer commented that 'Bock and Epstein offered two of the finer performances you will find this year' (Eck 1995: D5). The idea that this was a feminist version of the play arose primarily from Packer's casting of Corinna May in the villain's role, changing the name from Don Juan to Donna Gianna. She embodied, as Diana Henderson put it, 'the rebellious woman', smoking and cracking a whip while erotically drawing John Douglas Thompson's Borachio into her plot (1995: 16). Ben Brantley of *The New York Times* applauded the choice: 'Renamed Donna Gianna and played as a whip-wielding, nasty dominatrix by Corinna May, the character, with her snarling speeches about thwarted ambition, becomes as apt a figure of wronged womanhood as the maligned, virginal Hero (Kristin Wold), is' (1995: C13). Henderson was not convinced that the production, dubbed, 'exuberantly feminist' by *The Boston Globe* (1995: 35), deserved that appellation: 'what was apparently intended as a commentary on gender injustice instead came close to confirming stereotypes about unruly women once Gianna's villainy was directed at Hero and marriage' (Henderson 1995: 16). Henderson further wrote that 'the production celebrated unironically the goal of wedded bliss' with the result that 'structurally Gianna became the troublemaker who earned her subordination' (1995: 16). On the other hand, Henderson found the dynamic between Claudio and Hero poignant and moving. She remarked that Allyn Burrows's goofy shyness created unusual sympathy for Claudio, while Kristin Wold's Hero was 'indignant and angry, upset as well as embarrassed. She collapsed not from weakness but from the pain of betrayed love' (Henderson 1995: 16). What Henderson found especially noteworthy was how Packer 'contributed to the emotional tug of the plot' through immersive staging:

> While entrances from different areas in the woods added beauty and encouraged the audience's active attention throughout the evening, the wedding scene most fully exploited the outdoor seating. Down the center isle came the bridal party, prompting the audience to become part of the fictional scene while evoking those feelings we brought from our past attendance at weddings. The familiarity of this ritual added to the sense of shock when Claudio violated the ceremony, even before he attacked Hero. First, he briefly took over the Friar's position above, and, facing the father and daughter, signalled his presumption in becoming both accuser and judge. (1995: 16)

With the comedy of the wedding transformed into tragedy, Packer drew the audience into the play's funeral ritual. She staged Claudio's reading of the epitaph on Hero's tomb, scene 5.3, downstage near the front row. As Allyn Burrows's Claudio mourned, Kristin Wold's Hero could be seen in the distance, 'running through the woods in her white gown, a young woman debased by society, now free as a spirit, and perhaps an archetypal embodiment of the soul' (Packer 2022). As I have noted, Packer utilized the outdoor area to expand and expound upon the main action onstage with movement in the background. While enlarging the experience for the audience, these dumb shows, as it were, also attended to the actors' experiences of living inside the play. For Kristin Wold and her Hero, for example, the physical activity of running in the distance may have served as an energy release and salve following the devastation of the wedding scene.

In 1995 Packer also performed her *Women of Will* parts II and III in The Stables Theatre with Epstein as her scene partner. In 1996 she directed two productions, *Measure for Measure* in The Stables, and *Merry Wives of Windsor*, set in the wild west on the mainstage where she deftly wrangled her large cast of forty into a show that, as Iris Fanger wrote, 'remind[ed] us that the march of progress since 1600 has left out much improvement in human behavior' (1996: 50). Of the final scene, one critic wrote: 'The climactic set piece, in which Falstaff is tormented by townspeople disguised as ghosts and sprites, becomes a disarmingly sweet paean to the theatrical harmony Shakespeare always weaves from his comedies' chaos. One hopes, of course, that a similar spirit of reconciliation descends on the battling forces at the Mount.' (Brantley 1996: C11). Brantley was referring to the court battle between Edith Wharton Restoration, Inc. and Shakespeare & Company: 'That a resolution finally seems to be pending (a judge is expected to rule soon) has created its own, very evident drama as the company concludes its 19th season. The stage managers who introduce the productions (there were 15 this year) now make a point of saying that the theater troupe and the restoration are two separate entities' (1996: C11). Packer, as one reviewer wrote, 'was optimistic about the outcome of the case and her troupe's ability to work with the restoration group "to construct an inspiring plan for the property." She is offering her company's services to help raise money for the restoration' (Pincus 1996: H5). Like *Merry Wives* Packer's *Measure for Measure* indicated that human behaviour hasn't changed since Shakespeare's time, yet she ended both productions on a hopeful note.

Disturbing dichotomies: *Measure for Measure*, 1996

In 1996 Tina Packer mounted her second bare bard production, *Measure for Measure*, employing multiple casting to explore how the play challenges, and perhaps collapses the dichotomy between vice and virtue in human affairs. Seven actors played twenty-three roles. Every high-status reputedly virtuous character also played at least one low-status ostensibly unsavoury character. The set articulated the underlying hierarchies and oppositions that define virtue and vice in the play's Christian society while the casting and costumes complicated these simple distinctions. The production was among *The Boston Globe's* 'critics picks': Packer's 'pacing is terrific', noted the reviewer, who wrote that it was 'one of the most satisfying productions of the summer season in the Berkshires' (Siegel 1996: E 2). Another described it as a 'richly layered theatrical experience' in which 'Packer's top-notch acting ensemble plays these contrasts off each other in a dance that is as riveting as it is revealing' (Byrne 1996: Arts 1).[4]

The set design took advantage of existing structural features in The Stables theatre to create a layered unfolding of space that echoed the unfolding of the layers in the production's characters. Behind the long narrow main playing area were 'two large barn doors which, when slid open, revealed a smaller space upstage of the larger playing area, like an antechamber' (Wilson 2022b). Heaven and hell were represented in the outer playing area by two bands of carpet, stage right was blue for heaven; stage left, black for hell. Inside the antechamber upstage centre, a tall straight ladder simultaneously evoked Plato's Ladder of Love, the Great Chain of Being, and the choice between salvation and damnation: the upper rungs, painted white, led to heaven while the lower rungs, painted black, led to hell. Two short step ladders on either side suggested earthly aspirations leading nowhere. It was here in the antechamber that Angelo met Isabella, and here as well where the duke reached out to her in the play's final scene. The lighting, in dusky blues, created an atmosphere of suspension amid the stark horizontals and verticals of the carpets, ladders and doors.[5]

The casting and costumes, layered like the set, blurred dichotomies of heaven and hell, virtuous and depraved, implying that the seediest and simple might be the most humane. The play's physical spaces: court, convent, prison, brothel, garden, moated grange embody its examination respectively, of politics, religion, justice, prostitution, and seclusion. Packer's concept used multiple casting to demonstrate how the play collapses the distinctions among these places and concepts. As the actors switched among their roles, transforming into their opposites, the production visibly blurred the distinctions among these locations and their implied moral status. In this way Packer used the semiotics of casting to create for the audience a visceral experience of the play's moral and psychological complexity. As Ed Siegel of *The Boston Globe* put it, 'The hypocrisy, or double-sidedness of the moralists in "Measure for Measure" is highlighted by their appearing as more Falstaffian characters. The conceit works beautifully, as if puritanism inevitably leads to biological backlash' (1996: B8).

The production opened with all seven actors in the ensemble donning black cassocks, their veneer of virtue, as they processed on stage, chanting. They paused briefly before throwing off their robes, revealing the garb of their lower characters, and, perhaps, their ids: 'the bright and bawdy dress of prostitutes and pimps' (Byrne 1996: Arts 1). The rehearsal process, particularly *dropping in*, moved the actors through the emotional complexity, humour and revelation of embodying the high and low characters with their energy shifts, from sombre and staid to sexual and inhibited.

Johnny Lee Davenport, who is Black, played both Duke Vincentio, the 'fantastical duke of dark corners', and Elbow, the cuckolded Constable. Both are responsible for ensuring that justice is carried out while the competence of both is in question throughout the play. One reviewer wrote of his portrayal that his 'Duke is a genial one, played with a douse of common sense and good humor when he controls from a distance. Yet he proves ineffectual when faced with the emotional turmoil of Juliet and Claudio ... He runs from [Juliet's] tears, escaping on a quickly gestured blessing' (Mento 1996: 18).

Robin Hynek played both Mariana and Juliet, both of whom are victims of Angelo's self-righteousness. Hynek was also seen in the roles of Francisca the nun, and a nameless whore, roles that correspond to what would have been the only options left to Mariana and Juliet, having been ruined by Angelo. Allyn Burrows played Angelo as well as Abhorson, the executioner, and Froth, the tapster who cuckolds Elbow, lower characters whose social roles emphasized the darker aspects of Angelo's nature. Angelo orders Claudio's execution and attempts to cuckold God himself, as it were, with Isabella. Ironically, neither Abhorson nor Froth are abhorrent in themselves. This casting also resulted in broadening the comedy while underscoring the comparisons in scene 2.1, in the altercation between Elbow and Froth concerning Elbow's wife and in scene 4.3, the botched attempt to execute Barnardine. Both Angelo and Froth are in scene 2.1 at the same time. Packer handled this by having Froth represented by a stuffed dummy in the first part of the scene where he has only a few lines. Elbow (Johnny Lee Davenport, who was also the Duke) entered, carrying the dummy Froth, whom he arrested together with Pompey (Martin Asprey, who also played Claudio) for being 'two notorious benefactors' (2.1.54). As he arraigned them, he hung the dummy on the wall. Burrows's Angelo grew impatient with the tedious interrogation, and remarked that 'This will last out a night in Russia / When nights are longest there' (2.1.141–2). While making his exit on the line, he took dummy Froth off the wall, returning moments later dressed 'in the dummy's clothing' complete with a 'vapid grin and a silly voice' (Mento 1996: 18). The result was that the audience experienced a comic version of the trinity: Angelo, Froth and dummy. Packer's staging thus created stage images that illuminated for the audience the underlying impulses of both the Duke and Angelo, a point she reinforced by bringing Elbow's wife onstage, despite the fact that she is only mentioned in the text.

Kristin Wold played both Isabella and Elbow's wife. Packer created a brief dumb show of Wold as Elbow's wife, pregnant in a red chemise, sitting on Froth's (Burrows) lap thereby blurring the boundaries between Angelo and Isabella, Froth and Madame Elbow in the audience's imagination. Wold also played a nameless whore who appeared with Lucio and another whore in a stylized ménage à trois. The visual experience of seeing the same person who is the upright novitiate of the convent depicted as a whore, was intended to be disconcerting and suggestive for the audience. On the one hand it aligned Angelo's blackmail of Isabella with prostitution. On the other hand, it delved beneath the surface, as prompted by Shakespeare's invitation for us to wonder at Isabella's desire for 'a more strict restraint' (1.4.4). In working through Isabella's language, Wold noted that during *dropping in*, she wondered about Isabella's past:

> I'm generally in the camp that there's no subtext in Shakespeare. That what the characters are thinking and feeling is in alignment with what they are saying. And yet with Isabella, there is so much going on underneath in the unconscious that comes to the surface in these odd moments. There's shame for sure. Why does she go to the nunnery and why does she go to the strictest of all of the orders? I have a strong sense that if she's wanting that much order and strictness, it's because there's too much chaos. Maybe something was done to her or maybe it was her own behavior that she feels needs containment. (2022)

The play, as Packer notes, makes us wonder, 'what happened in this family?' (2020b). What matters, perhaps, is the question itself, the sense it creates of discomfort, of something dark, troubling and unacknowledged. This point was further developed in the doubling of Claudio and Pompey, played by Martin Jason Asprey. Claudio is arrested for committing fornication before marriage, implicitly prostituting Juliet, while Pompey, who works for Mistress Overdone, is in the business.

Meanwhile Mistress Overdone and Escalus, though occupying very different stations in Vienna's social and moral hierarchy, are, in Packer's view, two of the 'most humane characters in the play' (2020b). Both were played by Karen Beaumont, one of the company's clowns. Lucio refers to Overdone as 'Madame Mitigation' (1.2.40). While Lucio means a particular sort of mitigation, Escalus is also in the business of mitigation in that he is attempting to ameliorate the dire effects of Angelo's campaign to clean up Vienna. This double casting resulted in a poignant and funny moment when Mistress Overdone was arrested (3.2). Beaumont played both characters in conversation, switching back and forth until her Escalus ordered her Mistress Overdone to be taken to prison. As Escalus, she then called Lucio to be brought in for questioning regarding Mistress Overdone's allegation that he has had a child with Kate Keepdown.

Lucio was played by Walton Wilson who also played Barnardine, characters alike in their independence, nonchalance concerning justice, and lack of repentance. Lucio, dubbed a 'fantastic' in the cast list, refers to the duke as 'the fantastical duke of dark corners' (4.3.147), thereby inviting a comparison between them that Packer's casting reinforced. The two men, one white (Wilson), the other Black (Davenport), were of similar stature, both much larger than anyone else in the cast. Wilson played Lucio 'as a drag queen with a nasty sense of humor. At the time I was very large and muscled . . . I shaved my head and had a goatee, and I wore a lot of eye makeup' (2022a). He was 'draped in jewelry over a sleeveless diaphanous gown that was very flowy' and revealed his tattoos (2022a). Wilson recalled that he could feel the audience enjoying his 'comeuppance at the end … They loved to see Lucio finally get shut down in the fifth act. There was always lot of laughter at that. I played it as comedy. I always thought as Lucio I'd figure a way out of this. This situation is temporary whatever it is. I'll get back in the game soon enough. I never thought Lucio was actually repentant' (2022a). If Wilson's Lucio had no remorse, neither did Barnadine, whose perpetual inebriation was, ironically, also his salvation.

A welcome moment of broad comedy in the performance came when Asprey's Pompey and Burrows's Abhorson attempted to execute Wilson's Barnardine: 'Pompey swaggers in singing "Whistle While you Work" as Abhorson, with a Scottish burr, carries a gigantic ax and blows his nose on a bloody handkerchief' (Mento 1996: 18). They struggled with the intoxicated Barnardine, at last placing his head on the executioner's block. Abhorson swung the axe in the same instant that Barnardine, unawares, drunkenly raised his head and stumbled away. The drunken prisoner continued to inadvertently foil their efforts. Asprey's frustrated Pompey was preparing to smash Barnardine's head in with the chopping block when in walked Davenport's Duke. Asprey pretended he was lifting weights with the chopping block. The scene elicited raucous laughter from the audience. Yet, underneath the comedy was a more profound point owing to the casting. The doubling of Wilson as Lucio and Barnardine prompted the audience to consider what threat either one might pose to the social order. This contrasted with the doubling of Allyn Burrows as Angelo and Abhorson. The casting suggested that owing to his unexamined righteousness, Angelo, like his alter libido, Abhorson, was clumsy, ineffective and dangerous.

The production's heart was the sequence between Angelo and Isabella, unfolding across two scenes (2.2 and 2.4).

Each actor had a wrenching soliloquy. Burrows and Wold performed the devastating sequence with courage and raw emotion. Burrows's nuanced portrayal created unusual sympathy for Angelo. As Burrows sees it, Angelo has never experienced such powerful love (2023), while Kristin Wold explained that 'Isabella's language is often sensual, but she seems not to be aware of it, especially in the scene where Angelo falls in love with her. She keeps doing things that she doesn't perceive as provocative, but that's how he receives it, especially when she says she'll bribe him' (2021). Burrows said for him that was the 'turning point': 'He seizes on that word' (2021). 'How? Bribe me?' (2.2.149), he demanded, burning with anger. His anger exposed a knot of emotional and psychological complexity: suspicion and disappointment mingled with hope.

Burrows rendered a man in anguish as he wrestled with himself. Perhaps the most revealing moment for Angelo was when, following hard upon Wold's exit, Burrows's Angelo asked himself, 'What's this, what's this? Is this her fault or mine?' (2.2.170). As Burrows explained, in that moment, he was 'overwhelmed by a wash of love, a physical and emotional sensation all at once'. The line, 'What's this, what's this' meant to his Angelo, 'What is happening to me?; What have I found?; What is she doing to me?' (2023). For Burrows,

> Angelo was powerfully, sexually attracted to Isabella, and it caught him off guard. It was overwhelming. He's an emotionally crippled guy, and she made him feel whole in a way that he hadn't experienced, certainly not with Mariana. He loved her, and wanted to give himself over to her in spite of his position. He got carried away and then he was out of control. (2021)

In their second encounter, Burrows uttered Angelo's, 'I love you' as a startling, simple confession of love that seemed to surprise even him. His face was 'lined with pain' (Mento 1996: 18). In this moment Burrows's Angelo allowed himself to be vulnerable, possibly for the first time in his life: Burrows explained, 'In this moment Angelo is laid bare. He's in free fall. He knows at root that she can't or won't catch him, but that matters little. Nothing exists for him but Isabella' (2023).

Burrows reached out 'to touch her on an intense "Believe me", but she violently pull[ed] away as if from a viper' (Mento 1996: 18). The instant between Angelo's simple confession, 'Plainly conceive, I love you' (2.4.141), and Isabella's response holds an infinite number of possibilities. Yet as Burrows's Angelo knew, 'she could not or would not catch him' (2023). For Wold's Isabella, with her youth, her vulnerability, her desire for strict restraint, her fear for her brother, there was only one response. She was shattered, taken over by fear mixed with rage and disappointment. With her next breath, Wold's Isabella recovered her composure, pointing out his hypocrisy: 'My brother did love Juliet / And you tell me that he shall die for't' (2.4.143). Her sharp rejection caused Burrows to retreat from his exposed vulnerability into his position of power, taking revenge to cover his shame, becoming 'cold, authoritative' (Mento 1996: 18). Burrows's Angelo warned that he would 'give his sensual race the reign' as he 'wrestle[d] her to the ground ... forewarning but not fulfilling rape' (Mento 1996: 18). On the words, 'Answer me tomorrow' he knelt behind her, kissing 'her neck as her long hair cascade[d] down' (Mento 1996: 18).

Wold recalled that 'working on the second scene in rehearsal with Angelo was devastating but useful in terms of creating something that was raw' (2022). Of her soliloquy after her second meeting with Angelo, she said that she felt 'completely undone, emotionally devastated ... In our production, it was practically a rape – not an actual one, but it felt like my whole being was shattered. I was connected to visceral survival and in the vibratory state that comes out of that' (2022). The reviewer remarked on the realism and agony of Wold's performance: 'Kristin Wold's Isabella is electrifying' (Mento 1996: 18).

In Packer's production the encounter between Isabella and Angelo crystallized the play's excavation of the Christian opposition between spirituality and sexuality, high and low. These were two people faltering in the face of the combined force of sexual and spiritual energy, probing the wound at the centre of the play. Packer eschewed a definitive answer to the play's problematic ending by evoking one of the most well-known images of high Renaissance art, Michelangelo's *Creation of Adam*: 'The hands of God and Adam are dramatically frozen in time as if at any moment the world will explode when their fingertips touch' (artincontext 2022). The duke began to climb the ladder, upstage centre. Pausing, he turned and extended his hand to Isabella, who lifted hers towards him. Like the hands of God and Adam, dramatically frozen in time, 'a single shaft of light' captured 'their outstretched hands, suspended in mid-air, not quite touching' (Mento 1996: 18). Packer left it to the audience to absorb the final image: perhaps they would marry; perhaps Johnny Lee Davenport's Duke was in the role of God, breathing new life into Wold's Isabella; or perhaps he was seeking her help on the way to salvation. The image created by the specific actors embodying the roles opened up other resonances: Johnny Lee Davenport's tall, broad-shouldered Black duke reached out to Kristin Wold's slight of build, blonde and blue-eyed white Isabella, who reached out to him in return. Amid the play of these possibilities, Packer's allusion to the quintessential image of creation as inspiration – literally, an intake of breath in the moment before touch – is a reminder of the potential for beginning again with every breath we take.

Packer and co-director Kevin Coleman closed the company's second decade at The Mount with *Henry IV Part I*, 'swashbuckling Shakespeare' (*Boston Globe* 1997: C4), which received uniformly glowing reviews, owing to a strong cast of company members, stirring fight storytelling and a defining actor–audience moment:

> Epstein steals the show's finest moment – when he addresses the audience directly with his questions about the cost of honor. Sunday night's audience sat in silence as Epstein quizzed them, until they laughingly realized that he really wanted an answer. The moment, comic yet desperately serious, was the perfect foil for all the giant, impersonal actions taking place all over the grounds. It grabbed the crowd and brought them back to the center, reminding them that these were real lives being snuffed out in the name of ... in the name of what? ... Land? Title? Honor? (Eck 1997: B7)

The detailed setting complimented the action while the exquisite acting communicated the production's theme: 'As they fight for their supposed rights, it becomes clear that the wars will never end so long as men wear pride as a medal on their cloaks and hold honor more dear than each other's lives' (Fanger 1997: 36). The production also enfolded an ominous sign about the company's future at The Mount: 'John Pennoyer has scored a real coup by bracing up his craggy castle motifs with plain old metal scaffolding. The company's home ... is currently under restoration, and scaffolding is wrapped around much of the mansion ... Pennoyer's tongue-in-cheek design makes a motif out of a mess' (Eck 1997: B7).

Conclusion

In her second decade, Tina Packer developed her second style of staging Shakespeare, to wide acclaim. Her bare bard Shakespeare productions riveted audiences while engaging her actors in exciting new ways to explore Shakespeare's language and characters. Meanwhile, she continued to develop her grand mise en scène productions, imaginatively using the space to bring the audience into the worlds of her productions while inviting them to remain there with silent vignettes in the distance beyond the stage: Antony walking along with a soldier; Hero, running free, just visible in the distant twilight. Packer's continuing commitment to multicultural casting resulted in revelatory productions as well as training that contributed to the success of her actors' careers. Her 1989 *Tempest* had a white Caliban (Rocco Sisto) and a Black Ferdinand (Kenneth Ransom), and featured an amazingly courageous performance by Midori Nakamura as Ariel. Donning only her long hair and a loin cloth, Nakamura wove her magic about the estate as if she were native and indued unto the elements. *Midsummer Night's Dream* starred Kenneth Ransom who is Black doubling as Oberon and Theseus opposite Corinna May, who is white, doubling as Titania and Hippolyta, opening with a fight scene in which they were evenly matched. John Douglas Thompson, who is among the most revered classical actors in America, made his first appearance at the company as a show-stealing Borachio in *Much Ado about Nothing*.

The struggle over The Mount was heating up. Packer was hopeful that the company would be able to keep its home, the place where her vision of theatre took flight, borne on the rhythms of nature, balancing the harmonies, cultivated and wild, on an estate echoing in memory the grand country houses of her native England. Yet when it was time to look, not at visions but at realities, she could do that too.

3

What a dream was here![1]

Tina Packer opened her company's third decade in 1998 with *The Merchant of Venice* on the outdoor mainstage at The Mount, a controversial choice that ignited an extended debate in the community over whether or not it should be presented. I've reserved a full examination of that event for the next and final chapter of the book in order to pair it with her 2016 production of the play starring the same actor, Jonathan Epstein, as Shylock. This chapter explores how Packer used her artistic process to navigate change and examine the tangled knot of politics and war.

In 2001 the company left The Mount, having been out manoeuvred by Edith Wharton Restoration, Inc. in a lengthy arbitration. Packer moved her company to their new home on Kemble Street where she welcomed audiences with her staging of *Coriolanus* in rotation with Eleanor Holdridge's production of *The Tempest* at the same time the company was performing its farewell production, *A Midsummer Night's Dream*, on the outdoor mainstage at The Mount. Packer's 2001 *Dream* was a ritual farewell to the company's birthplace. Over one-hundred thousand visitors in total had made the trip to The Mount over the previous twenty-three years to enjoy the company's thirty-two mainstage Shakespeare performances, twenty-one of them directed by Packer. Of them all, her *Dream* exemplifies the quintessential summer magic of Shakespeare played outdoors by Shakespeare & Company.

Within two weeks of the company's farewell to The Mount came the September 11th attacks on the World Trade Center and the Pentagon, after which Packer's productions became more political. Her 2002 production of *Macbeth* incorporated images of political leaders across history and a soundscape that conjured modern warfare, while her 2005 production of *King John* explored a bitterly divided kingdom, deaf to the bitter lamentations of Constance and numb to the pathos of Arthur's death. These three productions form the centre of this chapter with in-depth case studies showing how Packer used theatre not merely to entertain but more significantly to work through personal and political trauma. I frame these analyses with surveys of *Richard III*, *Coriolanus* and *King Lear*.

In 1999 Packer directed *Richard III* indoors at the Duffin Theater in Lenox. Packer staged the women's laments in the play as a powerful form of protest that contributes to Richmond's victory at the end. Critics responded favourably, with one writing that 'The use of this device is stunning in its impact' (Koblenz 1999: C7). Ed Siegel of *The Boston Globe* found 'the battle of the sexes ... riveting' (Siegel 1999: E8); another wrote that Jonathan Epstein, who played the central role, was 'once again astonishing', and 'Packer's decisive and distinctive take' resulted in a 'Richard III' that was 'quite profound' (Sokol 1999: D13). One reviewer felt that the women's mourning distracted from the play's central interest, 'Richard's ability to charm, inveigle and otherwise persuade people to his side' (Byrne 1999: 3 Arts). There was no disagreement over her contemporary dress bare bard *Coriolanus*, performed by a cast of ten in 2000 in The Stables Theatre and remounted in 2001 to open Founders' Theatre: 'This extraordinary production is an example of Shakespeare & Company at its very best ... This is the perfect play for an election year, and Packer and her actors have given us a fine, thoughtful treatment of Shakespeare's portrayal of electoral politics' (Rozett 2000: 24).

Healing art:
A Midsummer Night's Dream, 2001

It was a sad day when Shakespeare & Company had to leave The Mount. The choice of *A Midsummer Night's Dream* as the farewell production was a natural one that gave the company the opportunity to say good-bye in the most appropriate and poignant way. It was known as the company's 'signature piece' (Gordon 2001: D1). As Packer remarked, 'It's the most ideal play for the outdoor woods of The Mount. The towering pines and undergrowth provide a magic which is impossible to reproduce in a conventional theater' (Tynan 2001: E1). The estate's expansive natural amphitheatre seemed uniquely designed for this particular company and Shakespeare's most exuberantly magical play.

The space shaped the company's performance style – athletic, exuberant, fearless. The company's unamplified voices resonated bell-like in the massive pastoral space: through the woods, stage left and right, from the balcony of the mansion and even when the actors had their backs to the audience. Jonathan Epstein explained that the space at once requires and permits 'enormous emotional and physical commitment' of a kind 'inappropriate in indoor theaters' (Gordon 2001: D1). The pine forest that hugged the mainstage had become a member of the company in its own right. It held the lights that illuminated the stage sixty feet below. It supported the actors that swung from its branches and leaned against its trunks.

Jim Youngerman, who designed the set for this production as well as many others, explained that his job as a designer was 'not to get in the way of the beauty of the space, which was perfect for *A Midsummer Night's Dream* – this moonlit stage with its front curve and multiple levels wrapped around with trees' (2022). His approach was to 'bring out the essence of place and scene' (2022).

The actors loved working in the space, despite the mosquitoes, because nature's energy fed their work. As Ariel

Bock, who has been with the company since the earliest days, mused:

> I can't imagine a more special place to perform Shakespeare: having my feet on the ground instead of a floor, and trees and the stars all around – it was beautiful and amazing. I think the audiences felt that too. They would stay from 8:00 to 11:00 p.m., sometimes even through the drizzle and the mosquitoes – let's not forget the mosquitoes. There was also the way the light changes as the summer wears on. In July we'd still be in daylight at the end of the first act, but then by mid-August we'd feel the summer ending: at 8:00 p.m. when the show started, it would be almost dark. There was a real sense of being in the hand of the rhythms of nature. (2021)

The rhythms of nature, earthly and celestial, are crucial to the resolution of *A Midsummer Night's Dream*. First the lovers, then the artisans, then Theseus and his hunting party discover themselves in the greenwood, presided over by Titania and Oberon. In this gradual crescendo of movement from court to wood the play's four plotlines coalesce into a healing brew as Hippolyta's opening lines foretell: 'Four days will quickly steep themselves in night: / Four nights will quickly dream away the time; / And then the moon, like to a silver bow / New bent in heaven, shall behold the night of our solemnities' (1.1.6–11). And somehow, 'four nights, magically become one' (Purcell 2023). The repetition of the word 'quickly' here, with its ancient Anglo-Saxon connotation, indicates that this rhythmic alignment is essential to life.

The choice of this play, then, was not merely fitting, it was vital. It gave the actors the opportunity to inhabit this play in this space one last time before it was gone forever. Packer's lodestar is her conviction that theatre can heal. Performance provides a means for addressing and moving through painful or difficult situations by clarifying and acknowledging them. *A Midsummer Night's Dream* is itself 'a healing play' according to Packer: It concludes with reconciliation after a series of power struggles between men and women in three different, overlapping realms: the political, Theseus and Hippolyta; the familial, Egeus and Hermia; and the supernatural, Oberon and Titania. These bitter conflicts echoed the extended struggle between Shakespeare & Company and Edith Wharton Restoration, Inc. Just as the play ends in reconciliation so Packer hoped the acrimony between the two organizations would fade as the Wharton Estate was restored and Shakespeare & Company moved on to new dreams in the heart of Lenox. That wish has been realized.[2]

If time has healed wounds, in 2001 they were fresh. Members of the company were barred from entering Wharton's house. Construction workers, who would bulldoze the mainstage after the final performance, were already at The Mount, so the actors found themselves rehearsing to the sound of groaning machinery. Rehearsals were the space for remembering and processing the company's imminent departure, and this became in a deep sense what the production was about. As explored in Chapter 2, one of the principal tenets of Shakespeare & Company's artistic practice is the importance of working from where you are, as you are – physically, emotionally and psychically – moment by moment. Out of this practice came the inspiration for Shakespeare's rude mechanicals to be contemporary construction workers renovating The Mount and doing work at the new property on Kemble Street. The company thus took aim at the current situation through comedy, revelling in the fun and release of speaking Shakespearean verse with exaggerated Boston accents to match their flannel shirts, hard hats, tool belts and work boots.

Tasked by Packer with doing the pre-show announcement, the rude mechanicals expanded the standard fare into what Jonathan Epstein described as a 'ten-minute lazzi' (2022b). They roared in on a pair of pickup trucks, 'one rusty red, one battered blue' (Tynan 2001: E1), with Kevin Coleman's Quince straggling behind on a bicycle that the actor, who is just over six feet tall, crashed into the blue truck every night of the run. After piling out of the pickups, they poked fun at everything that came to mind, 'riffing', as Epstein put it, on all the plays the company was producing that summer, including the usual pun on Coriolanus, and folding in a joke about the company's new theatre on Kemble Street, dubbed 'Flounders' (rather than Founders') Theatre. They worked in 'a few cracks about the restoration of The Mount ("So they finally got around to fixing it up when all those Shakespeare actors are outta here")' (Byrne 2001: 4), and concluded, pondering their task 'to collect some archetypes, because it's a lean and sterile promontory without a few good archetypes' (Epstein 2022b). One of the workers defined 'Archetype' as something 'like the Platonic ideal carrying a loaded bazooka' (Byrne 2001: 4). Here, the mechanicals were poking fun at Packer's concept of the play's frame as an archetypal struggle between Law and Love, embodied in Theseus and Hippolyta. Tom Yeager, who played Snout, asked, 'Where do you get an archetype?' Bottom knowingly replied, 'you got to examine the collective unconsciousness', after which they all looked at the audience for a while exchanging glances and asking each other, 'you got anything? ... no, you got anything?' (Epstein 2022b). Realizing they 'got nothing' from the audience (Epstein 2022b), they looked elsewhere, catching sight of Theseus and Hippolyta – played by Ariel Bock and Mel Cobb, standing on plinths like statues. They set them on stage, piled back into their pickups, and rumbled off with Quince straggling behind on his wobbly bike. Recalling two of Packer's previous productions, *The Winter's Tale* (1979) and her bare bard *Julius Caesar* (1993) the archetypes moved, stepped off their plinths and the play was on.

Mel Cobb's Theseus, draped in a toga underneath his armour, carried a large book titled 'The Law'. Ariel Bock was armoured as a warrior queen with 'wild hair' that embodied her wild nature and 'resistance' to 'patriarchy' (Rozett 2001: 20). Her Hippolyta, though conquered, did not relinquish her wildness. Rather, she defiantly opposed The Law with her archetypal embodiment of Love. When Cobb's Theseus and his hunting party came across the lovers in the wood, Bob Lohbauer's Egeus declared he wanted 'the law, the law'. Bock's Hippolyta strode over to the book and ripped out a page, presumably the one with the law that supported Egeus's claim. Rozett noted a significant ramification of the play's casting in this regard: 'the fact that Lysander is played by an African American actor and Demetrius by a white one suggests that the offending law may have upheld racial prejudice as well as patriarchal authority' (2001: 20). The Belle Epoque costuming of the young lovers deepened the historical juxtaposition between past and present.

Packer wanted the costumes to pay homage to the company's two decades at The Mount, honouring Edith Wharton's influence in art and literature. This design feature had the salutary effect of also illuminating the play's four plot lines. The rude mechanicals in their workman's garb addressed the present moment. The mature lovers embodied the conflict between Law and Love and the young lovers struggled with the unfathomable laws of love itself. Helena and Hermia wore lacy, layered Edwardian dresses in what was at once a nod to Edith Wharton and the sensibility of the play's courtship games. As Arthur Oliver explained, 'The [Belle Epoque] period setting of the court was Late Edwardian because Tina wanted to honour Edith Wharton' (2022a). Oliver noted that the layers of frills contributed to the comedy of the scenes as well as their significance in the unfolding story: 'what's funnier than watching some kids run off into the woods and scene by scene seeing those clothes break down, fall off, contribute to prat falls, entanglements, frustration – the costumes were the physical embodiment of what was going through the lover's minds' (2022a).

Elizabeth Aspenlieder, who played Hermia, explained that 'what came out during rehearsals was that my Hermia was very feisty, so the role became very physical as well' (2022). Tony Simotes, the company's fight master, directed the energy between Aspenlieder's Hermia and Samuel R. Gates's Lysander into acrobatic fights. As the layers of Edith Wharton propriety came off in the woods, the lovers became like 'barnyard animals', as Aspenlieder put it: 'There was a scene in which I come running down the hill looking for Lysander and I do a huge flip and fall into the dirt, every night. We all were filthy – doused with insect repellant and covered in pine needles and mud' (2022). Aspenlieder's Hermia donned Belle Epoque undergarments, accented by knee pads. In another moment, Lysander threw Hermia over his shoulder and she crawled down his backside. When 'Hermia wakes up to find Lysander gone, at first, she's in the middle of the forest, alone, in pitch black darkness. Then the lights in the tall pines come up and shine down on her. It was otherworldly' (2022). At the same time, true to Shakespeare, being in the show was also very much of this world:

> We're out there being drilled by mosquitoes, and you've got dirt in your nose and in your mouth, and you're sweating. And it's just, you know, it's live theater, man … With Tina and Tony (Simotes) you can't get away with anything but telling the truth. So you're actually going through these incredible highs and lows and betrayal, and fear, and elation, and love, and lust and jealousy and anger, and it all takes place over two hours … I lived a lifetime in those two hours. I felt Hermia become a woman. (2022)

While the lovers revealed their inner barnyard animals, the fairy kingdom was Elizabethan with notes of edgy Renaissance punk. The fairies, in skin-tone body suits 'adorned with wisps of fabric, straw horse tails, and horned stag headresses' were, 'sinister, sexually abandoned spirits' (Rozett 2001: 20). Along with Puck (Martin Asprey), in his 'grotesque makeup, long clawed fingernails on blackened hands, and Pan-inspired hairy leggings [they] emphasiz[ed] the dark unruliness of the woods' (Rozett 2001: 20). Titania's costume, Oliver explained, was inspired by Vivienne Westwood: 'She had a fitted glittering brocade Elizabethan bodice with open sleeves and a raffia skirt' (2022a). Allyn Burrows's Oberon wore leather pants, an Elizabethan jacket and a crown made of crow's feathers. He reminisced:

> It was a powerfully emotional, resonant time. The Mount was a magical place for me. When I showed up the company was only ten years old and already well established. I'd been there for twelve years when the company had to leave, but it still felt very new. It was a big deal for me to go out playing Oberon on that stage. (2021)

His Oberon was a 'spirit of the trees' with 'a huge rope suspended in the trees' from which he 'swung in at the top of the second act' (2021). One of the challenges of playing Oberon is to figure out how he becomes invisible. Burrows made himself invisible by saying 'brgh, I'm invisible' (2021) and remembered with pleasure how much he and Martin Asprey's Puck enjoyed the 'license to behave terribly' while invisible in the scenes with the lovers (2021). For his part, Asprey's Puck often took 'several tries' to cast his spells. The two were more comic duo than 'master and servant' (Rozett 2001: 20).

The fairies added an important dimension to the play's storytelling. Susan Dibble worked with them to build their world using Rudolf Laban's eight actions, creating a unique vocabulary of movement for each fairy: 'that became their language', she explained, 'because they don't really talk much' (2021). They sang beautiful Elizabethan harmonies as a chorus while the movement defined their individual natures: 'their movement was very specific and really interesting ... Each fairy worked within the world of their own movement within the world of other people's movement and, especially in the outdoor space, it felt authentic' (2021). Dibble found the rehearsal process 'very creative' and said the 'highlight' for her was working with 'a fantastic cast' (2021). She felt that 'as an ensemble, it was really the best I'd worked on' (2021). Rozett noted their work, commenting that 'the spirit world is filled with disconcerting sounds ... hissing and twittering and trilling and clicking' (2001: 20).

The music matched the production's generous expanse of design and emotion:

> The lovers' [piano] music becomes more agitated as the disorder among them intensifies ... There are some lovely Elizabethan vocal arrangements, as when the fairies lull Titania to sleep, and modern amplified music, with lively dancing when Oberon awakens Titania and invites her to 'rock the ground whereon these sleepers be'. The early morning arrival of Theseus and his hunting party is accompanied by a haunting cello solo. (Rozett 2001: 20)

Michael Gandolfi composed the music while Dan Cooper created the atmospheric sound, featuring rain-stick for atmospheric texture. Gandolfi recalled that Packer was deeply involved in shaping the music and sound for the production: 'She had her views as to where the different cues we wrote should be placed. There was a fluidity to the process: she would try things out before ultimately settling on a choice, and she found a place for everything. She showed a lot of respect for the composers and for the actors as well' (2022).

Gandolfi was surprised by the spontaneity of the rehearsal process:

> At one rehearsal when Dan and I had already done a lot of writing, Bottom needed a song for the moment just before Titania wakes, and Tina stopped the rehearsal. She said, 'oh, we need a song for Bottom here'. And she looked at me, and I was thinking, okay, I'll go home and compose a melody. And then I saw that all the actors were looking at me, and I realized oh – they want it right now. So I thought, well, here I go, and I made up a melody right there and sang the tune to Johnny Epstein. Then he got it and sang it. I loved that experience. (2022)

The production made references to the company's history at The Mount as well as its imminent departure. Because the actors were prohibited from entering the house, the terrace was off limits. Like the pine forest, the terrace had been an indelible aspect of the company's artistic vision and rhythm. As the previous chapters have shown, Packer used it for many productions. Its location behind the natural amphitheatre required the audience to turn around for the scenes that unfolded within its worn marble balustrade and on its zigzagging marble steps down to the green: it was the Athenian high ground where Theseus and Hippolyta looked over their realm; Romeo climbed its stones to touch Juliet's hand through its balusters; it was the storm-tossed ship that opened *The Tempest*. Since they were prohibited from using it for their farewell production, set designer Jim Youngerman recreated it on the mainstage. Stage right was a replica of the terrace complete with broken and worn balusters. Centre stage was a copy of the Edwardian French doors that exited onto the terrace from the dining room, 'carefully distressed and aged to mirror the original' (Oliver 2022d). Without the use of the actual terrace, the cast turned their attention to other ways to celebrate the outdoor setting, bringing it into the action:

> at the end of the lovers' long and confusing night, Demetrius and Lysander are throwing dirt and pine needles at each other, joined by a gleeful, invisible Puck. And the line 'You can never bring in a wall' [became] a response to the muscle-bound Snug's effort to move a piece of the New England stone wall that marks one end of the acting space. (Rozett 2001: 20)

The rude mechanicals stole the show and Bottom stole many a heart:

> Epstein, a fourteen-year veteran of the company with an astonishing range, brings his myth theory-spouting construction worker to life with great subtlety and humor. The other mechanicals cannot envision presenting their play without him; when he locks himself into his truck in a fit of pique because he cannot play the lion, they pound on the hood and windows and plead with him until he finally emerges. (Rozett 2001: 21)

Bottom was costumed as a carpet layer who made his entrance through the audience. Epstein recalled: 'I was carrying a carpet with my blue jeans almost halfway down my butt. When I walked in, everybody said "Bottom"' (2022b). Epstein, who clearly had affection for his character, continued:

> It wasn't that he wanted to hog the stage ... He was somebody who just totally loved language and the theatre and was capable of being moved by his own work in a real way ... He was surprised by his own eloquence, and he took himself really seriously, out of love, not vanity. Tina has a saying that 'the secret of comedy is to take your stupidity seriously – not to make fun of your character'. Bottom is the only character I've ever played whose drop looked the same as his triumph. He lost his sword in the woods, which put him 'in the drop'. So he flung his hand in the air to acknowledge it.[3] (2022b)

Bottom's dream was magnified into the company's dream of creating their theatre company at The Mount, a dream from which they were awakening. Epstein would fall silent after Bottom's line, 'I have had a most rare vision', and, as Rozett wrote, 'The woods fill[ed] with disembodied voices uttering famous lines from [Shakespeare's] plays' (2001: 21). The idea for this moment emerged in rehearsal as a way for the company's actors to perform their memories in the landscape that nurtured them and through which their voices had reverberated for nearly a quarter of a century. Every performance save the last used a recording played over speakers mounted on the spruce trees, sonorously evoking the company's collective dream in the open air.

On closing night, Bottom's dream was performed live by members of the company past and present, some of whom returned from far flung places to join in the final performance. When the sequence returned to Bottom for the closing lines (The eye of man hath not heard), Epstein found that 'it was almost impossible to speak. I don't know when I've been more moved' (2022b). Having played leading roles on the mainstage for the past thirteen years, he reflected on what it meant for him to play Bottom, who wanted to play all the roles and whose dream was the centrepiece of the company's farewell:

> In the context of the play, Bottom has seen a world that he knows nothing about, and it's going to change his life. His life will have magic in it from now on. In the context of the production, as a goodbye to The Mount, Bottom has had thirteen fertile years. From 1988 to 2001: I met and married my wife, we had our last child, and this is goodbye to the magic. And I remember literally hugging the big downstage tree that had become a good friend. That's the tree I swung from as Puck. It's the tree I hid behind as Benedick. It's the tree I leaned against during the wedding scene. It was with me in *As You Like It* in 1988 and 1990. It's a big deal that tree. And this is it for me working with that tree and for hearing these words ... The dream is ineffable. And consists of all these shared experiences. (2022b)

A Midsummer Night's Dream at The Mount in 2001 provided a means for the members of Shakespeare & Company to acknowledge and navigate the company's loss, transforming it into art shared with their audience. In performance they addressed their love for the space, for the words and the work, and they dreamt their dream of Shakespeare at The Mount for the last time. They danced amid the towering spruce trees for the last time. They felt the change of light that settles on the hills at dusk for the last time. They looked up at the stars in the night sky from the mainstage for the last time. Like the music of the hounds, Packer's production 'Seemed all one mutual cry' (4.1.114), making sweet thunder and laughter out of loss.

Within two weeks of the company's farewell to The Mount came the September 11 attacks. Shakespeare & Company had been planning comedies for the summer of 2002, the first official season at their new home. In the wake of 9/11, however, Tina Packer felt the company should reconsider its plans:

> I thought, whatever we do next season it hardly seems like comedy time ... It was a feeling that I'd never experienced in America. We couldn't escape the pictures of the towers coming down – they were on every television almost every minute of the day and night. We couldn't imagine what the implications were going to be, other than outrage and grief for those who died. We could hardly get through the emotional response to ask proper questions. (2020b)

Responding artistically to national trauma is a complex matter of timing, approach and style. On the one hand scheduling comedies for the summer may have seemed callous; on the other hand, producing a tragedy as dark as *Macbeth* was provocative summer fare less than a year since the attacks. Packer knew it was a risky choice. Yet, she mused, 'how do you let go of the darkness but by walking through it and really trying to examine it?' (2020b). As a theatre artist she needs to work on something that helps her navigate difficult feelings and ideas: 'I don't want to fight my mind. I need a play that gives me a way to hold all my own thinking about horrendous things happening on a national level' (2020b). In the months leading up to rehearsals she pondered the resonances between the contemporary political climate in America and Shakespeare's representation of eleventh-century Scotland. The result was a production exploring what drives the seemingly endless engine of war across time. Packer chose a contemporary setting to preclude romanticizing the play's brutality. She wanted the audience to see that 'the same desires run through the human race' now as then (Packer 2022).

Responding to national trauma: *Macbeth*, 2002

Set in post 9/11 America, only ten months after the attacks on the World Trade Center and the Pentagon, Packer's *Macbeth* began in enveloping darkness. One by one from all sides of the audience, the witches' queries filled the murk until, echoing through the theatre, they chanted in unison, 'Fair is foul, and foul is fair' (1.1.10). Their voices slowly diminished as they 'hovered through the fog and filthy air' (1.1.11), lingering, like a sigh. A surge of sound and light immersed the audience in the whop-whop-whop of helicopters, bursts of gunfire, and explosive flashes. Into this fog of contemporary war, the bloody captain (Martin Jason Asprey) appeared on the second-level upstage balcony in American Army battle dress uniform (BDU). He reported to Michael Hammond's grey-suited Duncan and Henry David Clarke's BDU-clad Malcolm, flanked by Banquo and Macduff, also clad in battle dress. Reporters with their backs to the audience skirted the stage, taking notes, photos and recording the speech. Secret service agents in trench coats lurked in the shadows.

The outer edge of the empty stage held scattered mounds of blood-red stones the size of human heads: silent witnesses to Macbeth's fear that 'Blood will have Blood / Stones have been known to move and trees to speak' (3.4.121–2). Red, the primary colour motif for the design, was repeated in the soldiers' red berets, Lady Macbeth's first appearance in a red suit and the red flowers on the golden kimono she wore in the murder scene, a visible echo of her boast that she would 'gild the faces of the grooms' with Duncan's blood (2.2.54), when Macbeth refused to do so, standing before her in anguish, stupefied, the blood on his hands matching the blood-red pattern of her kimono.

The cast of eight played multiple roles in Packer's bare bard style, crossing gender as well as age. Jennie Israel played

Lady Macduff, the gentlewoman, Donalbain and Seyton. Dan McCleary played Macbeth and the young Macduff. This casting created a pointed experience for the audience when Macbeth's order seemed to turn upon himself as young Macduff was murdered. Every cast member except Lady Macduff also played 'secret service agents', and every cast member except Macbeth also played the witches, who in this production were dubbed 'spirits'. Packer chose 'spirits' in place of 'witches', to avoid the distracting connotations of 'witch' for a contemporary audience while drawing on a key word from the play that embodies the complex, equivocal nature of the energy that moves through all the creatures in the world of the play.[4] Both within and without, Packer sees the spirits as energy – psychic, cosmic and natural – energy that permeates boundaries. At once sinister and satirical, the spirits embodied the equivocal, elemental energy of the 'unknowable, ungraspable machinations' that drive modern society (Packer 2020b). The spirits wore layered costumes so they could shape-shift quickly, transforming themselves according to Packer's concept that they were essentially a form of energy. Their outermost layer presented them as scientists in white lab coats. Beneath the lab coats the actors wore black body suits and underneath the bodysuits they donned racier disco attire for the cauldron scenes.

The witches in the play, '[kill] swine' (1.3.2) and dance around a cauldron, tossing in various animal parts, so in Packer's production the scientists in lab coats were one moment performing tests on animals in cages and the next breaking into song and dance routines, suggesting the 'sensational and escapist entertainment' that 'feeds our thoughtlessness' as a society (Packer 2020b). The magic of the witches, as Packer sees it, fundamentally derives from their information and knowledge. Neither good nor evil, they know more and possess greater awareness than everyone else, making them a force that, when harnessed by a character's basic urges and drives, can be potent and dangerous. In Packer's contemporary framework, science and technology, particularly in the form of media, become the 'magic' that wields power over peoples' lives. Packer sees the power of the media as unique in human history because of its scale (2020b). The spirits' energy seems beyond reach while at the same time it exists within the characters themselves.[5]

As she explains:

> The play lives on several levels. There are the things that happen in it; and then there are the images that haunt the play. These images work on the audience's unconscious minds, so that the most basic drives human beings have – for love, power, nurturing, and coupling – are awakened, and these basic drives forge a knowledge about ourselves that isn't always easy to accept. (2016: 233)

The most significant words in the play according to Packer are 'blood' and 'milk':

> These images are so potent in the imagination of the actors and audience (whether they realize it or not) because we are being called to our most fundamental selves – the selves that come out of the basic elements of life, the selves that want to be embodied, to feel ourselves in our bodies, that want to survive in *this* world, want to dominate in *this* world, want to unite blood and semen and milk in *this* world. (2016: 235)

The relationship between Macbeth and Lady Macbeth in the production exemplified these drives: 'Carolyn Roberts' Lady Macbeth is infantilized by her lack of identity until sexually turned on by the prospect of power' (Siegel 2002a: B2). Roberts's Lady Macbeth was young, beautiful and ambitious. One reviewer described her as 'fecund' (Ortiz 2002: D3), while another commented that 'Packer heightens the sexual compulsion between powerful McCleary and alluring, sensual Roberts' (Sokol 2002: D17). McCleary's guiding sense of

Macbeth's nature comes from Lady Macbeth's observation that he is 'too full of the milk of human kindness' (1.5.15):

> I started from that place of caring deeply about the preservation of my country and knowing I had married the only person I ever wanted to be with and was still sexually and romantically in love with, as well as having the privilege of a trusted best friend – and then having to let go of it all. Textually in the play, the actor has to let it all go really early in the story, but it must be the foundation so that Macbeth's conscience can play a role later as things spin out of control psychologically … It broke my heart to have to be none of the things I was at the beginning of the story. And so I let it break my heart as we played the play … I found ways to justify killing domestically that weren't demanded of me in war. And an actor probably can't play Macbeth if one is making all these mortal decisions without regretting one's own moral deterioration. (2022)

Packer's staging in the intimate playhouse brought actors and audience together, as one reviewer noted of McCleary's performance:

> We are steeped in Macbeth's thoughts and struggles between his heart and his head. This is no easily manipulated fool put up to an act of murder by his ambitious wife, but a thoughtful man, aware of his every move, fearful not of his enemies but of his resolve to act. McCleary's direct address to the audience, delivered with such open sincerity, somehow implicates us in Macbeth's deeds, making them more horrifying. (Byrne 2002: Arts 7)

The aching tragedy of McCleary's Macbeth had its antidote in Michael Hammond's porter, a highlight of the production. Hammond and Packer 'decided the porter would be a kind of Eddie Izzard style burned out, drugged out Vietnam vet, wearing a pair of women's silver pumps and speaking in a cockney accent' (Hammond 2022). When he first emerged through the trap door onto the stage the audience would laugh at the way he was dressed. He looked down, puzzled by his pumps. After a beat, he remembered what had happened only moments before he appeared, but kept it to himself and the audience would laugh even more. The porter's soliloquy became a fifteen-minute stand-up routine with Hammond improvising to explain the more obscure jokes in the scene and exchanging insults with the audience. The scene provided comic relief amid the intensity of the production. Yet, for all the fun of the moment, the representation of the porter as a Vietnam veteran, who had been subject to the draft, surrounded by the next generation of soldiers, who were volunteers, elicited a deeper, if implicit commentary on America's fraught relationship to its warriors and their different moral dilemmas. Packer further emphasized the painful ironies of America's military-industrial-research complex in the cauldron-apparition sequence (4.1; Figure 4).

FIGURE 4 *Macbeth (Dan McCleary) and Spirits (L-R: Henry David Clarke, Judith McSpadden, Carolyn Roberts, Michael Hammond, Jennie Israel, Martin J. Asprey, Johnny Lee Davenport). Photo: Kevin Sprague © Kevin Sprague, 2002. Reproduced with the permission of Kevin Sprague.*

Scientists in white lab coats entered chanting, 'double double toil and trouble', making notes as they set up laboratory experiments on caged animals. The sound of machines beeping and whirring encircled the audience. When Macbeth demanded to know if 'Banquo's issue' would 'ever Reign' (4.1.118–119), the show of eight Kings (SD 127) emerged as the voices of past and present leaders, Mussolini, Hitler and Bush – all calling their citizens to war. The voices surrounded the audience, echoing through the theatre. Then suddenly the sound shifted into a throbbing disco beat. The spirits stripped off their white lab jackets, transforming into scantily clad women and men, dancing erotically with Macbeth in the centre. Then they vanished, leaving Macbeth onstage alone.

This staging, with its calls to war by leaders around the world followed by throbbing music, suggested that much of our contemporary entertainment anaesthetises us to violence. Packer thus invited the audience to consider the similarities as well as the differences of war over time.

Tony Simotes, associate director for the production and company fight master, underscored the challenge of staging violence in the intimate space of the playhouse: 'If you swing a dagger or a spear on the Founders' stage it's in proximity to the audience' (Ortiz 2002: D 3). McCleary added that the 'Theater's Elizabethan-style seating configuration [makes] whatever violence appears onstage intensely intimate' (Ortiz 2002: D 3). Simotes finds in the play an exploration of the perennial question, 'What is our responsibility to violence?' (Ortiz 2002: D 3). The fight scenes descanted on the montage of leaders across time who justified war and called soldiers into battle. As Simotes explained, 'fight scenes, integral to Shakespeare's storytelling, continue the story through movement rather than words. The weapons and manner of the fighting reveal character' (2021). While Macduff and Macbeth carried automatic weapons in the production, they fought first with swords and then quarterstaffs. The sword, an emblem of manhood and the quarterstaff, an emblem of courage, served as reminders of the warrior, who 'Carved out his passage' (1.2.20), a passage that exemplifies Macbeth's skill in combat while presaging the ambition that turns him into a murderer. Yet, even as McCleary's Macbeth went 'beyond fear and shame' (Mento 2002: 17) in his horrific act of putting 'to th'edge o'th'sword / [Macduff's] wife, his babes, and all unfortunate souls / That trace him in his line' (4.1.167–8), he retained a shred of humanity for his hirelings in whom, perhaps, he saw himself: 'One of the most shattering touches comes when Macbeth pulls his hired thugs to their feet, giving dignity to men who will murder because they have nothing left to lose' (Byrne 2002: Arts 7). Packer explained that this moment emerged from the company's ethos, a habit ingrained in the rehearsal and training process: 'One of the principles of the company is nobody gets up off the floor alone, without someone offering to help. We encourage everyone to remain aware of others in the room and extend a hand' (2020b). In terms of the production itself, Packer reflected that the gesture enfolded an interpretation of what causes people to kill: 'What Dan McCleary, as well as Macbeth, understands, is that the people who are on the bottom of the pile are grateful to anybody who helps them. And he at least gives these men who murder, perhaps because they have nowhere to go, a touch of human dignity' (2020b).

Packer's production of *Macbeth* told the story of a sick country ravaged by war. It asked what drives us to kill while showing that, for all the courage and valour displayed in battle, killing empties us out. From this perspective, *Macbeth* is an anti-war play and Packer gave us an anti-war production at a time when the Bush administration was ramping up for its invasion of Iraq on 8 September 2002, not long after the closing performance.

The question of how and when to use art, drama in particular, to respond to national trauma is as old in the Western tradition as the Athenian theatre. Herodotus writes of the Greek tragic poet Phrynicus, whose play *The Capture of Miletus* caused 'the whole theater' to weep. The Athenians fined him 'a thousand drachmas for bringing to mind a calamity that affected them so personally and forbade the performance of the play forever' (1920: 6.21.10). Unlike *The Capture of Miletus*, which directly depicted the historic event, Packer's production was not a direct portrayal. Even so it came close enough to produce divided responses.

Dan McCleary recalled, 'it was a very risky production. It was met either with a very positive or very negative response. Sometimes we had people walk out on us' (2022). It's not clear why people left. Lenox audiences are accustomed to contemporary concept productions. It's possible it was too soon for audiences to process a production that referred to the political situation and trauma the country experienced, particularly those on the east coast. Founders' Theatre (now the Tina Packer Playhouse) is an intimate space that intensely focusses the energy. The production was relentless in drawing the audience into Macbeth's world, and the porter's scene provided the only comic relief.[6]

Like the audience, reviewers were divided. Two critics expressed dislike for concept productions in general, while one nevertheless found the production quality and performances strong:

> Despite the concept, it's hard to find fault with the production team or acting company. Mark Huang's sound design, especially, is magnificent, with speakers surrounding the audience in a swirl of noise and ethereal dialogue. Michael Hammond steals the show ... as a letter-perfect Duncan. This king is turned into a bureaucrat in Packer's vision; Hammond doesn't just wear a suit – he becomes one ... Dan McCleary ... is solid here, even in moments stuffed into a crisp white shirt ... Carolyn Roberts also is impressive as Lady Macbeth. (Eck 2002: D 4)

Another reviewer had difficulty with Dan McCleary's short-haired, clean-shaven American military general: 'I tend to see Macbeth as essentially a romantic rebel: long-haired, wild and violent, a throwback to a romantic, savage era of Scottish clans' (Santa Rita 2002: D4). This critique, which romanticizes Macbeth as a rebel rather than a murderer, would seem to prove Packer's point. If the savagery of warfare can remain safely in a wild and violent past of long-haired warriors, theatre-goers can avoid facing the perhaps more frightening way in which the rationalizations of leaders today drive the engines of war far from the killing fields.

Other critics praised the production. One acknowledged, 'this is not a production that will please those who prefer historical renditions of a classic' or 'those who do not like to have to think and interpret as they watch', and concluded that it was 'incredibly stimulating for these parlous times. Tina Packer and her most talented cast have gone out on a limb and are sawing through it near the trunk every time they go on stage' (Bass 2002: 48). Another appreciated its 'high-voltage', writing that 'eight' of the company's 'talented actors . . . stalk the two-tiered house during three hours of arresting theater' (Sokol 2002: D 17). This reviewer also appreciated the 'comic relief' in Michael Hammond's porter, whose 'point of view is singular, unsophisticated and most welcome' (Sokol 2002: D 17). The production was a critic's pick by Ed Siegel: 'Shakespeare & Company give modern-dress adaptations a good name with a powerful, emotionally direct interpretation by Tina Packer' (2002b: L3). In his longer review, Siegel critiqued the concept:

> Packer makes two controversial choices. One is brilliant – turning the three hags into a group of scientists whose approach to augury is something of a Manhattan project. The other is less so – by inserting the voices of contemporary leader-warriors as Macbeth approaches the battlefield, Packer ties the play too closely with the events of September 11, which she alludes to in her program notes. (2002a: B2)

For Siegel, *Macbeth* is 'more analogous to the '60s and Vietnam, which is why the Johnson-Nixon model fits so well' (2002a: B2). Siegel's review engages in the kind of substantive analysis that Packer wants her productions to prompt, for she sees theatre as an important engine of 'civil discourse' (Borak 2002: D2). The production was prescient in illuminating a world in which technology dominates our lives. Rather than giving us a romantic version of a long-ago era, Packer delved into the ways in which *Macbeth* continues to speak to us about the equivocal urges that drive us to war and the forces in our contemporary world that feed these urges.

The next year, in 2003, Packer continued her exploration of the roots of warfare. She directed *King Lear* with a cast of fourteen and a minimalist, out of time, design: all the costumes were in white and ecru, with bamboo curtains along the upstage wall and a plexiglass chair for Lear's throne. One critic noted that the energy of the actors 'spill[ed] over into the audience ... Packer's focus on raw emotion strips the play of artifice and gets to the heart of Shakespeare's tragedy. Her stunning take on "Lear" packs such an emotional wallop, you might be surprised that you've been holding your breath' (Byrne 2003: S7). Another wrote that it was 'an inspiring, distinctive "King Lear" [that] will long echo as director Tina Packer's voice is actualized through seasoned, stellar actors' (Sokol 2003: F14). The reviewer made note of the blend of accents on stage: 'Packer allows her actors to speak according to each individual's native dialect. Hence, Asprey and Malcolm Ingram (Kent) maintain British accents. Coleman, originally from the Midwest, maintains that geographical tenor. One might wonder at the lack of uniformity since pronunciation is evocative of country or region. The language differentiation, though, assists in character portrayal' (Sokol 2003: F14).

In contrast to the bare bard casting and contemporary design of the 2002 *Macbeth* and the bleached of colour ritualistic design of the 2003 *King Lear*, for *King John*, her next production on the theme of war and politics, Packer chose a large cast of eighteen and sumptuous period costumes. While differing in these material aspects of production, however, *King John's* sensibility is of a piece with the unorthodox twilight of *Macbeth* and *King Lear*.[7] Directing the play was Packer's first foray into working with a larger cast in Founders' Theatre while continuing her engagement with the political climate in America post 9/11. These three Shakespeare productions, staged in 2002, 2003 and 2005, form a trilogy commenting on America's political culture at the time. By 2005 America was engulfed in what became two extended wars in Afghanistan and Iraq.

The king's gambit: *King John*, 2005

Tina Packer's 2005 *King John* began with a dumb show as the lights came up on Arthur, Blanche and Henry playing with oversized chess pieces around a toy castle on the blue and red chessboard floor of the stage.[8] The screech of an electric guitar and throbbing drumbeat split the air as the children's game gave way to adult play: King John and his court strode onstage to the medieval-punk beat of Martin Best's original score 'strummed and drummed' (Fanger 2005: 20) live by three actor-musicians located on the upstage bridge of the playhouse (Barclay 2022). The prologue thus foretold the children as victims of the adults' war games, framing the action for the audience as a high stakes chess match that would determine England's future. Like the chessboard on the deep thrust stage, the costumes were in red (England) and blue (France), colour-coding that helped the audience follow the action.

While the set design was minimal, the costumes, designed by Arthur Oliver, were sumptuous. They evoked the play's time period with contemporary flourishes: Allyn Burrows's King John donned thigh-high red leather boots that might have come from Vivienne Westwood's shop in London. Mark Saturno's dauphin, like Burrows's King John, donned 'expensive foiled leather' (Oliver 2022a). Susannah Millonzi's Arthur wore a mail tunic that was 'quartered red and blue like the legendary King George' (Oliver 2022a). Barbara Sims's Constance was draped in a black crape dress with reams of yardage that accentuated her presence and particularly her lamentations. Annette Miller's Eleanor wore a fitted black velvet gown with a scarlet wimple around her head, and Peter Macon's Falconbridge, 'The Bastard', donned a jacket in 'parti-coloured fabric with contrasting gold paisley on black placed against a bold oxblood red and gold paisley on black' (Oliver 2023). Bobby Bigg's Austria wore a lion-skin draped over his back that Macon's Faulconbridge acquired by the end.

While overtly staging the play in the time period, Packer nudged the audience to pick up on contemporary resonances. She carefully chose period details that were theatrically dynamic: a curtained chair to transport the young Blanche onto the battlefield for the marriage truce with the dauphin; a cart for King John's agonizing death by poison. To these details were added pointed, if subtle contemporary references. In the Angers scene, for example, the audience could spy women in Afghan dress, an allusion to the Bush administration's invasion of Afghanistan.

Packer's chess motif served the production well, helping the audience follow the shifts in action. Mel Cobb's Cardinal, Packer noted, 'is a very big bloke, so every time he was on stage, his very bulk dominated the scene' (2020b; Figure 5).

Packer understood that amid all the back and forth between England and France and the city of Angers, it might be difficult for the audience to follow Pandulph's cold-blooded manipulation of their dispute, which brought them to heel under the Roman Catholic church. She staged monks in white-hooded robes lurking in the shadows around the edges of the stage throughout the play: 'From the first moment John was onstage, I had monks listening from the shadows, passing through, and around the edges of the action' (2020b). For King John's death scene, Burrows was wheeled on stage in a cart, writhing in pain from having been poisoned while 'three white hooded monks resembling the fates looked down from the balcony' (Mento 2006: 127). Without this context Packer sensed that the ending, in which King John is poisoned by a monk, would seem arbitrary. One reviewer criticized Packer for 'overplay[ing] the ecclesiastic imagery', but praised the

FIGURE 5 *King John (Allyn Burrows) and Cardinal Pandulph (Mel Cobb). Photo: Kevin Sprague © Kevin Sprague, 2002. Reproduced with the permission of Kevin Sprague.*

production's clarity: 'The hearty performances, especially that of Peter Macon as the Bastard, are refreshingly legible, and even the chaotic war scenes are rendered with brisk efficiency' (Brantley 2005: B 7).

Packer assembled a remarkable cast of company members and actors brought in through auditions to carry off her concept. Allyn Burrows played King John. Packer recalled: 'On the page, the Bastard is the attractive center of the play, but Allyn Burrows was bloody brilliant at John and he became the center of the production. He was funny. He turned his ignorance into comic bewilderment and braggadocio' (2020b). As Joan Mento wrote:

> After his atonement and submission to the Pope, he mockingly echoed the Cardinal's parting words, 'lay down [your] arms' and further snubbed him by dancing a jig. Yet, John's buffoonery was double-edged. As the scourged John, naked but for his robe, sat on his throne, the robe slipped slightly to reveal his nakedness. The picture of the half-robed King suggested vividly the decline of reason and power. (2006: 128)

Burrows credits Packer's directing for helping him create a King John that could centre the play:

> He's very mercurial and hard to pin down. I had to have personal stakes involved in navigating the exploration of that character. And she was really helpful in that ... She invites people to go further into those dark places or those absurd places and know that she'll be there on the other side to catch you. I trust her. (2021)

While Burrows's range as an actor helped him centre the play, Peter Macon's Philip Faulconbridge, the Bastard, was nevertheless a force to be reckoned with in a cast of exceptionally strong actors. Macon found that *dropping in* opened him to the psychological and emotional toll of his character's actions and words. He recalled in particular how rehearsing scenes through *dropping in* with two different actors led to distinct personal connections that deepened his performance. He and Walton Wilson, who played King Philip of France, were together in several scenes, one, a major fight scene. Wilson was his professor at the Yale School of Drama: 'It was great to drop in with him because then when we fought [as King Philip and the Bastard] there was heart and soul behind the desire to kill. *Dropping in* gave the violence and endowed the war with the reality of what it cost' (2022). Macon emphasized the importance of 'investigating the violence to that degree where it's actually meaningful and it's hurtful, it's heartful ... It cost me a lot to kill him' (2022). In contrast to Wilson, he didn't know Susannah Millonzi (Arthur) prior to rehearsal. His experience *dropping in* with her forged a strong personal connection with both her and her character that 'profoundly informed the commodity speech' (2022). Even though he and Millonzi 'didn't have that much to say to each other on stage', he was moved during *dropping in* by her 'vulnerability and innocence ... The process instilled in me paternal feelings, so that in the commodity speech, I was not only railing against capitalism, but also the future ... I found myself feeling very protective of her as a person and as the character on stage' (2022). Macon's performance earned plaudits: one wrote, 'This production catch[es] fire from Peter Macon's galvanic performance' (Borak 2005: Arts 1), and another described his Bastard as 'wild and brash and funny' adding that, 'as he must, he steals the show' (Kennedy 2005: C 5).

Susannah Millonzi was twenty-two when she played Arthur, but easily looked a decade younger, particularly with her hair cut short. Millonzi's relationship to the rest of the cast echoed that of Arthur's relationship to the characters in the play. She had grown up going to performances at Shakespeare & Company with her parents, an experience that influenced her decision to become an actor (2022). *Dropping in* helped her overcome her initial nervousness as a young actor surrounded by many of the experienced actors she had admired on stage. She 'immediately felt safe because everyone becomes steeped in the scenes together' (2022). As is the requirement for *dropping in*, she was present for all the scenes she was in, even when she had no lines: 'even though I didn't say much, I love those scenes. I was very present for everything that happened ... Because of the *dropping in* you learn the language and you learn your fellow players. You're looking them all in the eye and you're all there. Everyone is on the same page after *dropping in*' (2022). One of the most significant aspects of *dropping in* is the way it brings the cast together in a short period of time.

Packer staged Macon and Millonzi's characters, the Bastard and Arthur, as witnesses to the action. Macon's Bastard commanded the stage with long soliloquies and monologues. Millonzi's Arthur was mostly silent, yet that silence spoke volumes. Both characters were related to the play's centre, King John. Macon's Bastard was centred on the thrust stage amid the warring sides. For his soliloquies he could see every member of the audience with only slight changes of position as he spoke. In contrast to the commodity speech, which came easily to him, he had difficulty uttering the play's final lines. The fact that he was not alone on stage mitigated this discomfort, however, when he realized it was a public address, so it did not have to reflect how he actually felt. Even so, he struggled with the speech's celebration of England's nationalism and power. As he explained, there is an aspect of 'Shakespeare as a weapon' and the 'elitism that comes along with Shakespeare' (2022). As a Black American who had lived in West Africa and visited fortresses that held enslaved people, he had first-hand knowledge of the contrast between 'London–this incredibly gilded city with gold and marble everywhere–and these countries that that were raped and pillaged for the crown ... I had a bitter pill in my mouth about celebrating the glory of England when there's that to be answered to and reconciled' (2022). Then he realized that, 'if you compare the commodity speech and this final one, they're almost diametrically opposed. It's a great device in the play. You're watching the play through him the whole time, and he's criticizing everything that's going on. At the end of the play, who's left to say, not what we should think and feel, but to try to articulate the message. And who better should it come from, ironically, but the person who's been criticizing it?' (2022).

Whereas Macon's Bastard had numerous lines of direct address to the audience, Arthur's role was the opposite: 'He was there to bear witness and absorb what was happening from all sides, and, as a result would be sacrificed' (Millonzi 2022). Packer staged the scenes so that Millonzi's Arthur was often centred on the thrust stage, symbolic of his place, 'dead center in the middle of the politics' (Millonzi 2022). Millonzi recalled that, as Arthur, 'I felt fear coupled with awe. Everyone was fighting. I was jostled around a lot, and that physicality affected me internally, so I was constantly alert to the danger' (2022). Arthur's silent presence amid the warring factions of his relatives underscored Packer's thematic emphasis for the production.[9] At one point, Packer had King John and King Philip pushing Arthur back and forth between them: 'The ground was never stable. I felt desperation for my mother, but also real fear of her' (Millonzi 2022).

In the scene with Hubert (4.1), Millonzi's Arthur 'was trying to engage his compassion and empathy' (2022). She was taken with 'what strength of character this young boy had, to be able to make that appeal, and also to be able to jump … he comes from tough stock and could really hold his own when he needed to' (2022). Arthur's jump from the castle walls in scene 4.3 was performed on the ladder extending between the stage and the balcony upstage centre. The scene was both technically and emotionally challenging:

> I remember practicing the jump many times and we kept testing how far up I could be on that ladder to the balcony and feel comfortable jumping. I started the speech up on the platform and then I would come down the ladder and I would look down. The objective was to present the image of height to the eye of the audience, and then it would go to black and I would step down and then jump into the darkness. (2022)

Packer asked Clare Reidy, who worked with actors on *dropping in* as well as on individual scenes, to work with Millonzi: 'Clare helped me delight in the joy of it. She suggested to me, what if this is the best thing ever – that Arthur is liberating himself? What if this is everything? And that helped me crack it open with all the trepidation, fear, the height and the danger' (2002; Figure 6).

FIGURE 6 *Arthur (Susannah Millonzi) and Hubert (Kenajuan Bentley).* Photo: Kevin Sprague © Kevin Sprague, 2002. Reproduced with the permission of Kevin Sprague.

Packer's 2005 *King John* examined the cost of political greed and ambition for future generations. Her opening dumb show of children playing with chess pieces they knew nothing about was echoed in the production's closing moment. Meg Weider's Prince Henry dutifully watched his father die. As the lords in attendance knelt to him, shouting, 'God save the king' he stood silent in the same spot upstage centre where he had played with Arthur and Blanche at the beginning of the production.

King John is a history play with a historical narrative that lacks an overarching meaning. It is instead contingent, unpredictable and fragmented. The play thus has a philosophical and political relevance for contemporary America, an aspect of the production that reviewers noted: 'it is a work mired in the machinations of government of and by the sword. If that sounds a little too close to today's politics, you can be sure there are parallels between the plotting of King John and current events' (Eck 2005: D1). Louise Kennedy of *The Boston Globe* praised Burrows for his 'finely tuned ear and voice' finding a parallel between Burrows's 'childish, silly John who, frighteningly, wields deadly power' and the American president at the time. Kennedy did not name President Bush but instead made it clear with a long parenthetical remark: 'Any parallels to current political figures are intentional: note how the beleaguered people of Angiers [sic], pawns to John's political machinations, wear costumes evoking traditional Afghan dress' (2005: C5).

The production garnered praise. One critic wrote that Packer directs the play 'with vigorous grace' and provides 'heartbreaking insight into the costs of senseless war' (Kennedy 2005: C5). Another described the production as 'stirring', noting its contemporary parallels: 'Packer has mounted a drama that touches on issues concerning us today: the expediency of politicians who change sides as it suits their fortunes, the self-enhancing goals of religious leaders and the lone, thrilling voice of the common man, attempting to make sense of life-changing events he cannot alter' (Fanger 2005: 20). Ben Brantley wrote that Packer 'makes sure that we keep in mind who the ultimate victims are in a world where parental instincts turn warpingly political: the children. The boys, Arthur and Prince Henry (Meg Wieder), John's son, become the true emotional focal points – uncomprehending, terrified tools of power' (2005: B7). The production resonated with audiences and critics in 2005, who ascertained the play's relevance to America's interventionist global politics at the time.

Following her successful trilogy of political plays, Packer returned to the stage in 2006 as Gertrude in a production of *Hamlet* at Shakespeare & Company that was billed as a family affair, like the play itself. Her son Martin Jason Asprey was in the title role while her husband, Dennis Krausnick, played

Polonius. Directed by Eleanor Holdridge, who had worked with and learned from Packer as an assistant and associate director, the production was well-received, earning a detailed review in *The New York Times* that described Packer's Gertrude as a 'high-spirited, practical woman who would just as soon be pleasant as not but can push the power-queen buttons when crossed' (Brantley 2006: B 7). The reviewer for *The Boston Herald* described Packer as 'a lusty, good-natured Gertrude in love with her new king (played by Nigel Gore) and genuinely perplexed by her son's odd behavior' (Sanders 2006: 39). In 2007 Packer played Cleopatra in the playhouse now named for her. The local reviewer disliked what he described as her Cleopatra's 'giddy spring awakening in the early winter of her life' (Borak 2007: D3), while the reviewer for *The Boston Globe* described her performance as 'absolutely magnificent' (Kennedy 2007: C4).[10] The same year Packer directed *Coriolanus* with an all-male cast at the Mercury Theatre, Colchester, United Kingdom. While there, she made her first foray into performing her original theatre piece, 'Women of Will' for theatre audiences.

Conclusion

Tina Packer's third decade stands out in her oeuvre for the depth of her inquiry into what ails us as a society: sexism, racism, anti-Semitism, the thirst for power, hypocrisy and violence. In the wake of the company's move from The Mount to Kemble Street, Packer was able to stage productions in the new theatre space that would not have had the same visceral power outdoors. She adapted her bare bard style into a new style for the indoor playhouse, using smaller casts and minimalist set designs while taking advantage of the acoustics of the space and its state-of-the-art sound system. The most striking design feature of her playhouse style in this decade was her use of the stage floor area to crystallize the focus of the productions. In *Macbeth*, blood-red stones, the size of human heads, surrounded the stage like a silent chorus impinging upon the audiences' awareness. In *King John*, the chessboard floor, inviting a comparison between the children's game that opened the play and the cost of adult war games, did more than help the audience follow the action. It created a biting, if silent commentary that undercut the play's lofty speeches.

It's notable as well that with the turn of the twenty-first-century reviewers began to respond to and interpret Packer's multicultural casting. Martha Tuck Rozett, for example, astutely noted of the 2001 *Midsummer Night's Dream* that the sexist law invoked by Egeus was also racist. Packer endeavoured to make the worlds of her productions reflect our world. In her fourth decade this emphasis produced an original interpretation of *The Merchant of Venice*. Her 2016 production of the play fulfilled her long-standing conviction that Shakespeare's plays require a multicultural cast in order to speak to the complexities of our contemporary world.

4

Kol Nidre

The years 2008–17 comprised a time of return and renewal for Tina Packer. At the beginning of her fourth decade, she and the board agreed that she would step aside as artistic director after thirty years in order to ensure the continued success of the company under new leadership.[1] It was a propitious time to make the change. That year saw the grand opening of the state-of-the art Elayne Bernstein production and performing arts centre on the property, while over the previous three years, the company's ticket sales were among the highest in the company's history (Duckett 2008: D1). Under her new title, Founding Artistic Director, Packer has remained deeply involved in the company – holding regular meetings with the current artistic director, fund-raising, leading workshops and guiding projects that benefit from her stature and skill at large-scale analysis.

In her fourth decade Packer completed her monograph, *Women of Will* and took her show of the same name on tour across America and internationally, while directing eight Shakespeare productions at five different theatres. Her *All's Well That Ends Well* opened the 2008 season at the Tina Packer Playhouse to mixed reviews. Kristin Villanueva's Helena and Elizabeth Ingram's Countess earned plaudits, but many reviewers disliked Packer's troubadour concept, which turned Lavache into a modern-day songster akin to Bob Dylan. In 2010 she directed *Pericles* at the American Shakespeare Center and in 2012 she directed *Richard III* at the Colorado Shakespeare Festival, where it was billed as a 'vivid, suspenseful period production, directed by the legendary Tina Packer'.[2] With only four weeks of rehearsal time and a cast largely unknown to her, with the exception of Nigel Gore, who played Richard, Packer adapted her directing process. She changed her 'stumble through' after scene rehearsal into a 'stagger through' of the entire play on the first day with the cast (see introduction). It worked so well that she has done it this way ever since.[3] Packer was invited to direct several productions in Boston at *The Actor's Shakespeare Project* (ASP): *Troilus and Cressida* in 2012; *Henry VIII* in 2013; and *Henry VI Part 2* in 2015. Her *Henry VIII*, according to one reviewer, 'underscore[d] the precariousness and transience of power – and existence itself' (Aucoin 2013: G3). In 2014 her production of *Julius Caesar* opened in Lenox before travelling to Orlando, Florida and then to Prague, Czech Republic. In 2015 she returned to the ASP to direct *Henry 6 Part 2*, described as 'so much fun, it could make the "Henry VI" trilogy popular again' (Gantz 2015: G5). The final two productions of her fourth decade, *The Merchant of Venice* in 2016 and *Cymbeline* in 2017, were summer mainstage productions at the company's home in Lenox, Massachusetts.

The centre of this chapter is an examination of the two productions of *The Merchant of Venice* Packer directed nearly two decades apart. I demonstrate the adaptability and success of her methods in different rehearsal circumstances and venues. The 1998 production was performed outdoors on the expansive outdoor mainstage at The Mount with a cast of forty-four in her grand mise en scène style, with eight weeks of rehearsal to opening night. The 2016 production was staged indoors in the round in the playhouse named for her with a cast of fourteen in her playhouse style and only four weeks to opening. These two productions differ significantly in scale and rehearsal time while exemplifying the dynamism of Packer's collaborative approach to directing. If the 1998 production demonstrated the fulfilment of her artistry in a large-scale outdoor production, the 2016 production realized the ways her work with a smaller cast indoors elicited unique interpretations with a multicultural cast. In the nearly two decades that passed between these two productions, the socio-historical context in America and in the Berkshires had changed. In 1998 when the company announced the play as among its summer offerings, some in the community wrote to the local paper trying to prevent it from being performed. In 2016 however, there was no controversy. Perhaps Packer's sensitive handling of the controversy in 1998 as well as her thoughtful staging of the play changed some minds. The same highly esteemed actor, Jonathan Epstein, played Shylock in both productions, and his singing of the Kol Nidre gave voice to an important dimension of Judaism. The world was different in many ways, perhaps the most significant being that, in addition to America's strain of anti-Semitism, the Black Lives Matter movement had reignited the concerns of the civil rights movement. While Packer's 1998 production focussed primarily on the problem of anti-Semitism and sexism, in 2016, her multicultural cast brought to the fore the trauma of the Black experience in America as well.

Prologue

Tina Packer had long eschewed directing *The Merchant of Venice* because she 'never wanted to do a play with such layers of bigotry' (Gover 1998: 7). Yet, that changed when she 'went on a huge reading binge' (Gover 1998: 7), which included James Shapiro's *Shakespeare and the Jews*, inspiring her to imagine staging the play in all its complexity. Visiting Venice gave her a 'visceral sense of the ancient city's teeming history of multiculturalism centred on trade and profit' (Packer 2020c). And Jonathan Epstein, one of her most versatile leading actors, who was Jewish, wanted to play Shylock: 'I was an ambitious actor, it was obviously a pretty good role for me, and I was interested in the play' (2021). Even as Packer overcame her own reservations about the play, however, she encountered resistance, first from the company's board and then from the Berkshire community.

At Shakespeare & Company's board meeting in 1997, Epstein recalled, 'Tina introduced the idea of doing "Merchant" as more or less, here's what we're going to do' (2021). The board did not have artistic authority, even so, they began debating whether or not the company should stage what some strongly felt was an anti-Semitic play. One board member suggested they vote on whether or not to have a vote on whether or not they should produce the play. Over the objections of one board member who said they couldn't vote and another who cautioned, 'this isn't a board meeting … this isn't a board meeting', they ended up taking the vote on whether or not to vote on doing the production. 'It's the most Jewish thing the board's ever done', Epstein quipped (2021). The vote on whether or not to vote on doing the production did not pass. Packer moved forward with her plan to make *The Merchant of Venice* the centrepiece of the 1998 mainstage summer season. She saw the play as relevant: 'as our lives today are increasingly about trade, business and prejudice' (Gover 1998: 7). Even so, the board meeting underscored Packer's deeply felt responsibility to be sensitive to the play's complex reputation and history, issues that were raised by concerned citizens when Shakespeare & Company announced its 1998 summer season.

Addressing these concerns was her next challenge. On 7 May she and Epstein attended the monthly meeting of the Jewish Federation of the Berkshires to answer questions about the upcoming production. That visit may have assuaged the concerns of some, but it did not prevent a series of letters from appearing in *The Berkshire Eagle*, the local Lenox paper, over the next two months. The drama that played itself out on the pages of *The Berkshire Eagle*, as Edward Rothstein put it, was 'rehearsing the familiar historical debates about this play' (1998: E2). Some letters defended the play for its depiction of Shylock as a complex character and a great role for an actor. Others pointed out how the repetition of Shylock's most volatile aspects has been used to foment hatred against the Jews, 'codif[ing] anti-Semitic caricature' (Rothstein 1998: E-2).[4]

Collectively, the letters addressed what is at stake any time the play is performed. Both the play and the Venetian ghetto, Shaul Bassi observes, are 'fundamentally ambivalent documents of Western Civilization, having been both instruments of intolerance and catalysts of and for cross-cultural understanding, vehicles of antisemitism and portals of knowledge of and sympathy for the Jews' (2016). For James Shapiro this is why 'censoring the play is *always* more dangerous than staging it':

> To avert our gaze from what the play reveals about the relationship between cultural myths and people's identities will not make irrational and exclusionary attitudes disappear. Indeed, these darker impulses remain so elusive, so hard to identify in the normal course of things, that only in instances like productions of this play do we get to glimpse these cultural fault lines. ([1996] 2016: 228)

Accordingly, the 1998 production 'came out of the context of real heartburning about whether or not it was the kind of play one could do at all' (Epstein 2021). Packer sees theatre as the very place to work through difficult problems, so she turned controversy into opportunity. As part of the summer programming, she led a 'Discussion Series' in the early evenings prior to performances, bringing together actors, scholars and teachers with playgoers, on topics ranging from 'The Role of Jews in a Slave Society' to 'The Myths and Realities of Venetian Economics' (Gover 1998: 7).

The play had many of the elements that drew Packer to Shakespeare in the first place; it presents conflicting ideas without resolving them, and it explores family relationships: 'the play is also about fathers attempting to control their daughters and is comprised of three love stories, each of which turns out to be fraught in its own way' (Packer 2020a). On the one hand the play anatomizes anti-Semitism at its ugliest; on the other hand, it reaches across religious difference in exposing the patriarchal family structure that treats women as commodities. Further, like the bond between Shylock and Antonio, all of the relationships in the play prove to be transactional. After the heady passions of attraction comes the trauma of the courtroom, rippling through Shylock and Antonio and the three young couples: 'everything is negotiated to a certain level, and when the play ends we are left feeling that those negotiations are for the moment only' (Packer 2020b). Underlying the transaction between Shylock and Antonio, Packer observed, is the charged intimacy found in Shakespeare's warriors. Like the battles between Hal and Hotspur, Coriolanus and Aufidius, the violence underwriting the bond between Antonio and Shylock, expresses how the two merchants feed on one another, indeed, how they need each other to define themselves: the bond they agree to is, as Packer put it, 'not a merry jest at all – it's throwing down the gauntlet' (Packer 2020c).

The play explores how love, hate, religious and racial tensions are inextricably bound up with each other in a city where trade and finance are held together in structural tension by the law that enables them to trade. Beneath that edifice, Packer emphasizes, are the enslaved people of Venice, whom Shylock invokes in the courtroom scene to underscore the hypocrisy of the Christians (4.1.89–100). In creating the world of the play, this detail was crucial to Packer's vision. She kept the enslaved in the audience's awareness throughout the performance, employing the company's recent training programme graduates in multiple roles, including the enslaved, who moved stage properties between scenes and hovered abject at the edge of the action.

Creating Venice at The Mount, 1998

The expansive outdoor stage at The Mount was well-suited for creating the world of the play, alternating between the bustling streets of Venice and the airy opulence of Belmont. Venice occupied two-thirds of the playing space, stage right. Belmont was situated stage left across a bridge that joined the two while also serving as a 'tableau space' (Mento 1998: 17). For Venice, Packer used music, movement and pageantry to establish the mise en scène, manifesting how the three monotheistic faiths coexisted more or less peaceably in the Mediterranean port city. The performance opened with the Muslim call to prayer and closed with Epstein's Shylock chanting the Kol Nidre. In between Christian monks chanted *Dona Nobis Pacem* as they wove their way through throngs of merchants, prostitutes and the enslaved. The sacred songs descanted on the secular law that allowed the three religions to coexist in the tenuous peace that profited the city.

Every evening of the performance as the audience settled in on the lawn, the sound of a single voice in Arabic floated on the evening air. It was the Muslim '*fajr*', a prayer chanted before sunrise, marking the break of day. Within moments came a rush of activity as the enslaved of Venice appeared, setting up stalls on the Rialto, with its merchants, bankers, moneylenders and venders. Next came the doge, played by John Douglas Thompson, at the head of a procession followed by Christians, Muslims and Jews. His appearance brought everything to a halt. As he crossed the stage, everyone genuflected, making 'it clear that the doge had the power and that his power derived from Venice's position at the head of a tripartite alliance of Catholics, Muslims, and Jews' (Epstein 2021). There were 'hooded figures, inquisitors, robed in black who would wander around. Suddenly a character would be brought face-to-face with them ... showing how dangerous it was for the Jews in Shylock's community' (Randolph 2021) because they feared being arrested if discovered outside the

Ghetto after curfew. This staging emerged from the 'Who is a Jew' exercise that I discuss shortly. It portrayed the extremes of the city's quotidian life of commerce, from the high ceremony of the doge's procession to the labour of the enslaved.

Belmont had its signature movement and music as well. Choreographer Susan Dibble used the spacious outdoor green designated as the beautiful mountain to create 'a vocabulary of movement that was between dance and gesture' (2022a). The movement offered a serene, ritualistic celebration of femininity as Portia's gentlewomen in flowing gowns moved rhythmically, raising first their right then their left arms in graceful unison. Dibble explained that

> the arm movement came out of exploring with the actors in rehearsal, and was similar to tossing a ball of yarn or a very light ball. I was inspired by the quality of Isadora Duncan's dance, having studied her technique. The emphasis was on the flow and weight of the women's bodies, and their costumes made it possible to capture the movements beautifully. (2022a)

Their two-layered gowns were created by costume designer Arthur Oliver with 'heaps of yardage' in rayon, 'so there was a lightness to the volume' (2022b). Each dress was in a different shade of 'muted earth tones, from soft grey to patterned beige', complimenting the overall costume colour scheme of black, white, and red, while 'the trick of the dresses is that they could transform depending on how the top layer was worn' (2022b). When the top layer was draped over the head, it gave 'the wearer a very nun like look' (2022b). For the grand processions led by the doge, with a simple flip of this layer over their heads, the actors playing Portia's gentlewomen were transformed into novitiates, bowing in prayer as the doge passed by.

In between these extremes were the wanton, 'feckless youths', as Packer called them, who associated with

Malcolm Ingram's Antonio and Peter Wittrock's Bassanio (2020b). These were Solario and the 'Sals', as Packer referred to the three actors sharing the role of Salario: two men, Ty Skelton and Michael Toomey and one woman, Tori Rhoades (2020b). The innovation manifested how sacred and profane brushed up against one another in Venice and more subtly in the play, not only in terms of commerce but also with respect to sexual exchange and marriage. With three Sals rather than one, Epstein's Shylock was outnumbered in scene 3.1 when they mocked and abused him. This staging encouraged the audience to comprehend the cruelty of the scene as expressed in its language. Solario was played by Jenna Ware as a courtesan in a red dress with an enormous whip. The two male Sals, Michael Toomey and Ty Skelton were costumed as male prostitutes: Toomey wore a corset with a tutu around his neck; Skelton donned 'a ruff over a loosely draped open front jacket that accentuated his alabaster skin' (Oliver 2022c). Tori Rhoades was arrayed as a courtesan in a 'red rouched polonaise with a white ruff' over a corset (2022c). All three were in white face, giving them a sinister, carnivalesque, edge. Jenna Ware's Solario could roam the streets of Venice with the Sals, interacting freely with Bassanio and Antonio, while Tod Randolph's Portia stood veiled in a white dress on pedestal in Belmont awaiting her suitors' choices. This contrast underscored Portia's plight, while adding another layer of ambivalence to the world of Packer's Venice.

Moving inside the world of the play

Packer had an extensive schedule to guide her large cast through the complex dynamics of the play. Two exercises invited the actors to explore and experience the play's manifestation of anti-Semitism, racism and sexism and the hierarchical structure of multicultural Venice. The company's movement exercises begin with the guideline 'to move about the space' and are accompanied by music that begins and pauses movement. The exercises progress in stages, moving from basic to more complex.

Who is a Jew?

This exercise was inspired by James Shapiro's discussion of Jews in Britain and the anxieties circulating in early modern England with respect to Christian as well as Jewish identity. The exercise progressed in stages that raised the stakes gradually. Once the actors were accustomed to moving through the space, starting and stopping according to the music, they were asked to make eye contact when they encountered someone. In the next stage, they greeted those they encountered. Finally, they were asked to improvise, speaking briefly before moving on. After this warm-up, the more detailed exercise in religious-ethnic identity began.

The exercise had two parts. For the first part the cast drew lots that assigned their religious identities as either Jewish or Christian. If an actor drew a token assigning a Jewish identity, the objective, Jonathan Epstein explained, 'was to see if you could figure out who else was a Jew, while not revealing that you were, in fact, a Jew, to anybody who wasn't' (2021). The second stage of the exercise asked each actor to decide on their own whether or not they were Jewish. In this stage, if an actor chose to be Jewish, they could reveal their identity or decide to be a crypto-Jew, hiding the fact from everyone except other Jews, as in stage one of the exercise. As the actors moved about the space and greeted each other, then spoke, they improvised their conversations, each with their own private intention. The exercise invited the cast to experience what it felt like to live in a world where hiding or revealing religious identity is fraught and possibly dangerous, a threatening world that demands careful choices in terms of when and how to reveal one's identity. A second exercise helped the cast experience viscerally the play's fluid shifts in status and power among the characters.

Who has the power?

This exercise, called 'The Power Walk', encouraged the cast to explore different types of power and status among and between Shakespeare's characters in the play. It was designed to help the actors develop an embodied awareness of the many complex connections and hierarchies in the play. Packer uses 'the five ps' to think about power: political, personal, psychological, poetical and physical. The number of 'ps' increases or decreases depending on the play. *The Merchant of Venice*, for example, has at least six 'ps' since Shylock has pecuniary power over Antonio for part of the play. The guideline for the exercise was to move through the space, and as you encountered someone, to follow that person if their character has power over your character at any time in the play. For example, as the doge, John Douglas Thompson had the most political power, so everyone in the cast would end up following him at some point in the exercise. There are other modes of power in the play that cut across race, gender and religion. For example, both Jonathan Epstein's Shylock and Malcolm Ingram's Antonio followed Tod Randolph's disguised Portia who had power over them in the courtroom scene. Ingram's Antonio followed Epstein's Shylock who had pecuniary power over him. Epstein's Shylock, in turn, followed Ingram's Antonio, who had power over his sentencing in the courtroom scene. As Portia, Tod Randolpn's power walk took her from standing on a pedestal entrapped by her father's will to standing in the courtroom, where, for a few moments, she was the most powerful person in the play.

An exercise such as this can help to generate innate responses that become second nature during the life of the performance. Packer wants her actors to be alive in their bodies and in tune with their breath, responding viscerally and spontaneously as they move about the room and then into performance. After all exercises, the cast circles up to discuss what they discovered, focussing on how it felt rather than what they thought. These discoveries are everything from feelings and sensations to new understandings of their characters and relationships. They might reveal interpretations of the text as well, but that is only one among a myriad of moments that help bring the actors into the play's world. Packer's process is generative: she wants to build embodied experiences and relationships that shape the energy of the performance. The large-scale exercises take place after *dropping in* and before or in rotation with scene work. Of the many discoveries that occurred during *dropping in* and scene rehearsal for this play, three provide examples of Packer's synergistic way of directing.

Shaping scenes

2.7: *Morocco, A dignified prince*

The choice to understand the interaction between Portia and Morocco not as one of racist revulsion on Portia's part but rather as an attraction that she hid from her gentlewoman, Nerissa, emerged from *dropping in*. Tod Randolph, who played Portia, explained, 'This was the first time that I worked with John Douglas Thompson … and we ended up playing a genuine attraction between the two of us. It was very sad when he gave the wrong answer because he was obviously very young, handsome and sexy' (Randolph 2021). Packer supported the choice, particularly because Thompson was doubling as the doge: 'Having John Douglas Thompson in both those roles, with his regal presence, was terrific. Morocco for him was not comic in any way. He was romantically heroic' (2020a). They decided not to cut Portia's line, 'Let all of his complexion choose me so' (2.7.79); instead, Randolph said it in a way that made it clear she was dissembling with Annette Miller's Nerissa. If Morocco had chosen the right casket, Portia would have no choice but to marry him because of her father's will. Yet openly avowing attraction for someone of a different race and religion was taboo in that society.

Portia's attraction to two of the three suitors added poignancy to her plight, reinforcing the fact that, even as different religions and races coexisted in Venice for the sake of commerce, this was not a society equally accepting of all creeds and cultures. Nerissa had her secrets as well: Miller, who is Jewish, played Nerissa as a Marrano. Packer positioned her so that she could be seen in the distance lighting Shabbat candles then furtively snuffing them out. Such secrets between even those purportedly as close as mistress and gentlewoman aptly capture the complexity of the historical time period as well as the play (Figure 7).

Portia's second suitor, Dan McCleary's Aragon, was outlandishly comic, appearing before her with an extraordinarily long train carried by two pages. As one reviewer wrote, 'The moments of comic relief ... are hilariously comic and quite a relief' (Eck 1998: B7). McCleary doubled as Old Gobbo with Martin Asprey as Launcelot Gobbo. Together they played the comedy to the hilt.

FIGURE 7 *Nerissa (Annette Miller) Portia (Tod Randolph), and Prince of Morocco (John Douglas Thompson) with ensemble in. Photo: Neil Hammer. Reproduced with the permission of Stephen Ball, Shakespeare & Company.*

3.1: The mad scene

Jonathan Epstein refers to scene 3.1 as 'the mad scene' because Shylock is both angry and mad with grief. The scene opened with the sound of Shylock's cries, 'echoing through the city' (Mento 1998: 17). Epstein's Shylock entered, his long grey hair tousled, in a loose white robe, clutching his daughter Jessica's dress. The three Sals wrenched the dress away from him, tossing it among them as they mocked and kicked him, laughing with the crowd that formed to watch. The scene, visceral and frightening, was staged during scene rehearsal after excruciating *dropping in* sessions. Some of the actors found it painful to utter the hate-filled taunts in the scene. A conversation ensued when Jonathan Epstein explained that, as an actor, he needed the hatred to fuel his response. He needed the Sals to be as vicious as possible in order to incite his rage and grief while making his state of mind and heart comprehensible to the audience. Packer encouraged the actors to work through these feelings, explaining that the viciousness serves the show, the audience, the other actors and most importantly Shylock. As Tod Randolph recalled, Packer always set aside time 'to discuss our personal experience as actors, entering into a violent, a hate-filled moment, and to be able to discuss that openly. Tina always gave actors that opportunity, as did directors trained by her' (2021). Packer encourages her actors to go as deeply as possible, but she does not push them. She is there to help them understand that the work is in the service of creating theatre that illuminates who we are and what we do, from our ability to be compassionate and merciful on the one hand, to our tendency towards self-interest and cruelty on the other.

4.1: Which is the merchant here, and which the Jew?

The courtroom scene brings together the play's two plots, juxtaposing the different predicaments of Shylock and Portia disguised as Balthazar. Epstein explained that as Shylock, he appeared in court 'as a Venetian merchant ... I set aside my Jewishness' (Borak 1998: D1). Epstein 'did not want to play the role for sympathy ... I thought, this is a man who behaves really badly. And I didn't want any limit on how badly I could behave, but that would only be the case if it were clear that I was doing this, not because I was a Jew but in spite of it' (2021). To underscore this point Packer staged the trial scene with a significant presence of the Jewish community in Venice. Shylock's desire for revenge, Epstein explained, 'horrifies the other Jews, who fear reprisal. They are trying to get Shylock back to the idea of sufferance being best for the tribe' (Borak 1998: D1). Packer saw Shylock's desire for revenge as a means of 'swapping one kind of pain for another' (Borak 1998: D1). This leads to the mystery of Portia's behaviour in the courtroom. In Packer's and Randolph's reading of the scene, Portia follows her lovely speech about the quality of mercy, with a relentless pursuit of justice against Shylock to the point where it begins to feel like revenge. Perhaps it was born of her inability to elicit compassion from Shylock. Both Packer and Epstein thought Portia wanted to move him. As Packer explained:

> She's naive enough to believe her speech, the quality of mercy, will ... be enough to make Shylock merciful. She does not understand how revenge will bring psychic relief to Shylock. The law upholds those who are in power. ... Shylock is an alien even though he was born in Venice and Jews lived there for centuries. What happens to Portia is that she sees the world in a different fashion. (Borak 1998: D1)

Epstein added, 'She's talking about being big-hearted to someone whose heart is broken and mad' (Borak 1998: D1). While the trial scene is a place of reckoning for Shylock, Tod Randolph experienced a significant shift in Portia's comportment to the world, recalling that 'the role of Portia really stretched me, emotionally and technically' (2021):

> I was playing Portia as a member of this wider society, that Portia had no immunity from this prejudice against Jews, that it was just as much a part of her as it was of everybody else. Antonio's a Christian and I'm not going to let him be killed by a Jew. What sets Portia apart is that she gives Shylock an opportunity to change his mind before coming down on him with what she knows. This was something I found for myself, going from wearing the white dress, standing on the pedestal, my father controlling my life from beyond the grave, to being dressed as a man and enjoying the power that comes with that. After the courtroom scene, the dress I wore when I came home in the very last scene was essentially the same design as the white one, but in red. It still had a very tight bodice, so that hadn't changed. It was still extremely feminine. But the red color suggested something had been unleashed – something of blood, of sexuality, of maturity, of stepping into womanhood, stepping into power, stepping into a completely different relationship to men, to my husband. After the courtroom, I had shifted with regard to all of these elements. (2021)

Ed Siegel of *The Boston Globe* wrote that Randolph's 'performance ... rivals Epstein's', in delivering 'a Portia who is wise, witty, self-sacrificing, and noble, but also vain, sometimes cruel, racist, and anti-Semitic' (1998: C8).

4.1.388: I am content

In the courtroom scene Jonathan Epstein struggled with Shylock's response to Portia's question, 'Art thou contented, Jew? What dost thou say?' (4.1.388):

Now there's a whole lot of things Shylock might be. He might be beaten, he might be planning revenge, he might be hopeful ... But of all the many things he might be, content is not one of them ... The basic principle of Tina's productions is you mean exactly what you say at a deep level all the time ... I couldn't figure out any way to say 'I am content' and mean it ... We had several long discussions about it. She said, 'do you want to cut it?' I said, 'no, of course I don't want to cut it. I just can't solve it'. So she said, 'well, just say it loudly'. So I said it loudly. Still not knowing what it meant. And of all the many things that I did in that production, that's the one that comes up the most. People will still come up to me and say, 'you know what I really remember about that production? Was when you said "I am content ... I knew exactly what you meant"' (2021).

Packer gave Epstein the option of not having to say the line. Since he didn't want to cut it, she took a different tack. Her suggestion to 'say it loudly' derived from her knowledge that the voice can hold opposing truths simultaneously: 'The physical attributes of the voice when speaking loudly help create a pathway of sound. In making a big statement, the actor finds a way to mean it while also betraying himself. A larger, louder statement can hold both truths' (2023a). She didn't explain this to him at the time, with the result that the quandary remained alive in his body and voice, becoming Shylock's as well. In saying it loudly, Epstein's Shylock betrayed himself, meaning it and not meaning it. Sometimes saying it loudly is the most effective way to respond to a question that is really a trap.

Kol Nidre

The Kol Nidre came up in rehearsal when Packer asked Epstein if he wanted to sing the Khaddish, the Jewish mourning prayer. Epstein responded by singing the Kol Nidre for her. She immediately felt the power of the Hebrew and Aramaic declaration and wanted to use it. The question was where to place it. Packer wanted to retain the play's comic ending, so she placed it moments before the lovers' reckoning over the rings. Epstein chanted it offstage right in the dark from behind a wall, so that the audience could hear but not see him. The chanting of the Kol Nidre for Epstein's Shylock was deeply personal. In reciting it, he felt he was an 'echo of all Jews' (2023b). In the distance, Christina Calfas's Jessica joined in.

The haunting chant proved too powerful to be contained: 'Despite the romantic comedy of the rings in the last scene, [the] production leaves the audience with a stage image that reinforces the tragic dimension' (Mento 1998: 18). Edward Rothstein wrote: 'Kol Nidre declares null and void all rash oaths and bonds made to God during the year, including, perhaps, Shylock's forced conversion. The prayer's inclusion signalled the production's recognition of an injustice latent in Venetian justice' (1998: E2).[5] Another reviewer declared, 'You will not forget Epstein's performance ... his final wail, as he chants ... will linger with you for a long time' (Eck 1998: B7).

The production was an artistic success. It was an audacious choice for the opening of her third decade at The Mount, particularly in view of the controversy it provoked prior to opening night. Packer turned controversy into conversation with her well-attended pre-show discussions of the play. More than that, she knew that in Jonathan Epstein she had an actor capable of embodying Shylock in all his complexity: he was witty, clever, conniving, tender, hurt, funny, broken-hearted, enraged, mad with grief and finally resilient. The audience felt that resilience as his voice reached them in the dark, under the open sky filled with stars.

Of Packer's 1998 production, Ed Siegel wrote, 'What [Packer] has done is present a multilayered portrait of a multicultural society torn apart by ethno-centrist hating. She has gone beyond any simplistic notions of personal good and evil toward a dissection of the psychic and social price paid from Bosnia to Crown Heights when ethnic division defines personal identity' (5 August 1998: C8). The same could be said of her 2016 production.

Memory theatre: *Merchant* in the round, 2016

If Packer's 1998 *Merchant* created a world, her 2016 production responded to the world, grappling with how the past haunts and shapes the present four-hundred years after Shakespeare's death. Past and present were juxtaposed in the design, music and soundscape as well as in the actors' performances. Emblazoned across the stage floor was a white cross superimposed on an image of the Seal of Solomon. Written on the white cross in black script were passages from Amelia Lanier Bassano's 'Defense of Eve'. These words of the past, a history of over a millennium compressed in layers on the stage floor, were answered by words from the present written in black on white banners covering the facings of the first balcony. They formed the 'Memory Theatre', which began as a rehearsal exercise inspired by Frances Yates's book, *The Art of Memory* (1966). Packer and the cast decided to make them part of the set. In the collective experience of the theatre space, the words are secret, yet shared: 'The play is about secrets. Every character in the play has layers of secrets. The memory theatre exercise was about expressing something personal and fixing it to the theatre space' (Packer 2022). They were words from recent American tragedies: 'I can't breathe'; 'Black Lives Matter'. From politics: 'Progressive thought'. From poetry: 'A tree scarred still bears ripe fruit'; 'transcend'. From Shakespeare: 'My tongue will tell the anger of my heart'; 'O why should wrath be mute and fury dumb?' Shahar Isaac recalled that what he wrote was positioned on a balcony facing so that he could see it as he entered the courtroom scene: 'the beginning of that scene was very much driven by that phrase' (2022). As Packer explained:

> The play is about our memories – years of collective and individual memories of the holocaust. More than half the audience in Lenox is Jewish. These layers of memory, these vibrations of the psyche are about our connections to each other. The words on the paper are there for the audience to see and reflect on or not. Whether or not someone thinks about them consciously, they still affect the imagination. (2022)

The performance began with maskers just visible in twilight, a haunting redolent of narrow Venetian alleyways underscored by the play's central sound motif, a 'thumping' that would intensify and then submerge, evoking a sense of 'night-time, darkness, and oily water … something distasteful and unseen moving through' the world of the play, 'the heartbeat of all the ugliness and horror' (Levy 2022). The thumping segued into the heartbeat of Bruno Mars' 'Uptown Funk' as the stage burst into a disco party beneath flashing globes hung from the theatre's 'heavens'. Over the course of the play, the spheres, evoking Venetian blown glass, transformed from the disco strobes of the opening into the celestial spheres of Lorenzo's speech in the play's final scene. The maskers wore elaborate gilded masks dotted with jewels, with bird's beaks or glitter, and elegant late Elizabethan garments in rich velvet. As they fell in a heap after the dance party, the audience saw that they were Antonio, Bassanio, Gratiano and the three Sals, one of whom was a woman. In contrast to her 1998 production, Packer did not want any ambiguity with respect to the nature of Antonio's relationship with Bassanio: Hadden's Antonio rose and stood aloof for a moment then returned to pull Bassanio up from the heap into a passionate embrace, emblematic of their relationship and the financial rescue that would set the play in motion. Over the course of the play Antonio's elegant black and gold brocade velvet jacket grew threadbare while Bassanio's became more elaborate. The Sals donned periwinkle velvet. Cloteal Horne's Sal began in a dress and subsequently changed to poufy breaches to align with the shift in her gender she experienced when she joined with the other Sals in the mocking of Shylock. Packer used the same approach as in 1998 staging, with the Sals tossing Jessica's dress back and forth between them. As Horne recalled:

> Because of the *dropping in* work, I had a close visceral relationship with [Hadden's Antonio]. I wanted to support him. I was loyal … There would be times when it felt so intense … It was hard to go there because of the level of hatred and violence that had to course through my body and the bodies around me, particularly in those two scenes [where the Sals torment Shylock] … It was complex, too, because of the three of us, I was the only fem identified body, and I was constantly trying to understand my role as a feminine essence amongst those male bodies, and my depth of loyalty, patriotism almost, undying allegiance: how is that different funneling through my Black fem body? It was powerful to experience that level of rage and unnerving as well. (2022)

The music moved back through time as well, beginning with Daniel Levy's throbbing arrangement of Bruno Mars' hit song, followed by Christian, Muslim, and Jewish calls to prayer as the lighting slowly brightened into dawn, transporting the audience from the very American scene of the disco into Venice's world. As the composer explained, 'Packer wanted to use the religious music to walk us through the streets as the world was waking up while the party animals were lying on the stage' (Levy 2022). The production closed with a galliard, the traditional Renaissance jig: Monteverdi's lively 'Damigella tutta bela'. Along the way Levy's setting for 'Fancy's Knell' invited actors and audience alike to step outside of time, pondering along with the cast, 'Why do we want this? ... What makes us want someone?' (Levy 2022). Packer staged the moment as a lyric pause while Shahar Isaac's Bassanio was considering which casket to choose in scene 3.2. She had the cast turn outward towards the audience to sing the song. The song complimented the staging as a contemplative moment for everyone in the theatre, as Levy explained:

> 'Fancy's Knell' opens with a harp gently repeating two notes. The harmonies that follow are jazzy in their complexity. But the questioning lyrics, unresolved harmonies and glowing, harp-propelled accompaniment bring the audience to a sense of longing and ambiguity: an unanswered question. Like many theater songs, Fancy's Knell covers a lot of emotional ground in a very short amount of time, and ends as the actors sing a joyful death-knell to Fancy herself, finally landing on another unresolved chord. We've just taken an unexpected and energized inner-monologue detour, but have landed back in the main story, and the narrative balloon remains in the air. (Levy 2023)[6]

Every detail of the production intertwined present and past, from the multicultural cast to the enslaved people of Venice woven through the scenes. As in the 1998 production, Packer made the enslaved an onstage presence, helping the audience to experience the hypocrisy of Shakespeare's Christian Venice while keeping her cast constantly in motion as they changed between their characters and the enslaved. In 1998, with her large stage, she used supernumeraries to perform the enslaved. In contrast, for her 2016 production, she used most of her fourteen cast members to embody the roles in a manner akin to her bare bard productions. The result was that nearly the entire cast held the play, switching between their characters' individualized identities and those of the nameless multitudes that undergirded Venice's powerful place in the Mediterranean. The masks of the enslaved changed throughout the production.

Sometimes the cast wore simple white theatre masks, in other moments they took on the most grotesque stereotypes of Jews, Muslims, and Blacks, and in still other moments they were mysterious, veiled women, a visual reminder of how the play's fathers attempt to control their daughters. Most of the cast was constantly shifting positions between their more privileged, individualized characters to experiencing what it felt like to be transformed into chattel once they donned the masks. When the entire cast holds the play in this manner, the constant shifting of energy between roles keeps the actors alive in their bodies, creating vibrations felt by the audience in the intimate space.

This seamless unity suggests a director's concept framed and communicated to the actors on the first day of rehearsal, particularly given the short rehearsal period of only four weeks to opening night. But the opposite was true. Even with the short rehearsal schedule, Packer held fast to her principle that 'the creative energy of the actors is what makes plays work' (Packer 2020c). The resulting production was a collective effort guided by Packer's keen presence, gentle prompting, and inquisitive approach. The production embodied the principles upon which she founded her company: a desire to go deeper into the complex problems of Shakespeare's plays with a multicultural, international cast. She ensured that the artistic crew and associate directors reflected the cast's diversity. Noa Egozi, who, like Shahar Isaac is Jewish and from Israel, was an associate director along with Raphael Massie, who is a Black American, as were three of her actors, Thomas Brazzle, Deaon Griffin-Pressley and Cloteal Horne. Every aspect of the final production of the 2016 *Merchant*, from the shaping of scenes and the characters' stories to the set, costume design, and music, emerged from her rehearsal process with the cast. With her rehearsal time half of what it was in 1998, Packer followed the adapted approach she had been using since 2012, when she changed the stumble through to a stagger through.

Energizing the circle: The stagger through[7]

When the cast showed up for rehearsal the first day, they found chairs set in a circle on the stage of the Tina Packer Playhouse. This circle was the safe space for the cast's twice daily check-ins at the start and close of each day. For the next two days, it was the arena for the cast to run, leap, laugh, and cry their way through the entire play. This was not a 'read-through' or a version of 'table work'. It was 'a stagger-through'. The guidelines were simple. Packer told the cast: 'when it is time for your scene, get up on your feet and go! Let your body take the impulse. Play. Be Brave. No shame, no blame. If you don't know your lines, we will feed them to you'. Packer had her associate directors ready with the script to 'feed in' the text if the actors needed it. Bella Merlin, who played Nerissa, recalled:

> As much as this process is absolutely terrifying, it's actually fabulous. Because it's so instant the body and the feelings have to do most of the work … You can't help but take risks … There is the joy of working the play on its feet in the knowledge that you can't fail. You're invited to just dive in, do what you want, go where you want, see what happens … When John Hadden's Antonio was asked for the pound of flesh, he took his shirt off. There was a sudden awareness of one semi-naked body on its knees surrounded by all these fully-clothed people. We instantly felt the visceral shock of where this scene might go. (2021)

The 'stagger through' encouraged active, embodied and instinctive responses. They jumped up when it was time for their scenes and returned to their chairs, shifting between performing for and watching their cast mates. This generated a deeply ludic and fluid exchange of energy, awareness, playfulness and trust that drew the cast together within a few hours. Regular discussions and 'check-ins' deepened and maintained this creative energy and trust throughout the rehearsal process. The day before the first rehearsal Packer emailed a prompt, asking the cast to think about identity: how they identify themselves, why identity is important, and what that means with respect to belonging to a tribe or a community. Beginning with these first two days and continuing throughout the rehearsal process, Packer invited the cast to discuss what was happening in the room before or after scheduled breaks as well as at the start and close of each day. The questions Packer asked focussed on feelings and images rather than ideas. The most frequent question was: 'what came up for you in that moment?' As I explained in the introduction, the circle is the safe space for the cast to talk about what comes up throughout the rehearsal process. In that space the cast goes deep. Shahar Isaac recalled: 'Tina comes with her heart on the plate, and you don't want to do anything less than that. You want to give your heart to her, and to meet her where she meets you ... She is so much about making sure the actors are in the right state of mind and heart and spirit' (2022). Cast members are invited to discuss anything and everything that influences the process of bringing the play to life.

Energizing words: *Dropping in*

After the 'stagger through', Packer spent the next two weeks with the cast *dropping in* the entire play. While the 'stagger-through' involved the entire cast going through the play together with actors leaping to their feet when it was time for their scene, *dropping in* took place between scene partners sitting in chairs, knees almost touching, maintaining eye contact. Packer uses her associate directors to help with *dropping in* in the play, giving them hands-on experience in her approach to directing. It was the first time several actors in the cast had experienced *dropping in* an entire play. In their words the process was 'profound', 'magic', 'amazing', 'deep'.

The intensive process of *dropping in* forges connections between the individual actors and the language of their characters, as well as between actors. They find and develop their characters' stories through a deep, personal connection with Shakespeare's text. Merlin found *dropping in* to be 'time efficient' because 'by the end of those seven days the cast knows more about the play than after three weeks of regular rehearsal' (2021).

Packer's guidance to the cast was to keep expanding, keep moving and stay open to new insights, not only throughout the process of rehearsal but the performance run as well. She suggested they keep journals to chart their character's journeys. As Isaac remarked: 'She's not a director that would come a month in and say, "What is this? This is completely different than what we rehearsed." No, she creates a playing field that allows you to keep playing and discovering' (Isaac 2022). The sense of a shared history and the personalization of the text created through *dropping in* were further developed in the scene rehearsals, addressing questions that have engaged scholars, students and actors for generations: Why does Antonio lend Bassanio money and why is he willing to die for him? Why does Bassanio turn to Antonio in the first place, and whom does he love: Portia or Antonio? Why does Portia suddenly turn on Shylock with such venom only moments after she has expounded upon the quality of Christian mercy? Shakespeare's texts have an expansiveness that invites multiple answers to these questions. Through *dropping in* the actors find their own answers. Once Packer sees where the actors' energy is taking them with their character and their relationships, she makes adjustments by asking questions and making suggestions as necessary, She rarely tells them to do something specific because she wants the actors to have agency over their characters and the creative process.

Raphael Massie admired the way Packer guided her multicultural cast through what were emotionally challenging rehearsals of a play that explores ugly human behaviour during the summer of 2016:

> I do not want to understate the importance of how Tina set the room for the process. It was largely unspoken, but there was an understanding among all of us with respect to how challenging this story was going to be to tell and how uncomfortable it was going to make us and how uncomfortable it was going to make audiences. And there was an unspoken agreement that we were going to make our way through that discomfort in the hopes of representing a story that could impact audiences rather than just doing a play. We all know the concerns that go along with the *Merchant of Venice* with the Jewish community in particular. Because of the way the play was cast, we were able to tell a more robust story about oppression and marginalization as a whole and still keep the story focused around Shylock. (2022)

The scene work, like *dropping in*, was broken down by beats. As with *dropping in*, Packer's associate directors worked on the scenes with the actors so that several could be rehearsed simultaneously. In rotation with the scene rehearsal schedule, the company's movement and fight artists, Susan Dibble, Kristin Wold (movement) and Jonathan Croy (fight), rehearsed with actors on specific moments and beats. Packer focussed her attention where she felt it was needed most, staying in touch with the cast through the morning check-ins, while sometimes adding evening check-ins as necessary. Two moments in the rehearsal process stand out for demonstrating how Packer's approach gives actors agency over creating their characters, resulting in unique, profound performances.

Portia

Tamara Hickey, who played Portia, reflected, 'I always felt a level of shame and guilt [as Portia] because her journey has so much to do with the desire for agency and power, and then when she gets it, she sees how easily she can cause harm' (2021). Hickey acknowledged that her Portia had an edge to her: 'she felt like someone who was trying to turn her circumstances into an opportunity, or to somehow benefit from them, turn things around' (2021). At the same time, however, she was also a young woman who, as she began to taste degrees of freedom, was always about to veer out of control. Hickey felt her Portia was akin to a 'caged animal' because 'she's been held captive her whole life by her father' (2021). Hickey noted that the only power Portia has had is with Nerissa, who is her confidante and gentlewoman, and that for them, the power is all play: 'she's toyed with this idea of having power' but with Nerissa, there are really no stakes: 'it's just a game' (2021). In contrast, when she arrived in the courtroom, Hickey's Portia suddenly found herself not only engaging with power in the world, but in a situation where the stakes were life and death. Her disguise – costumed as a male law clerk – had a surprising, disconcerting effect on her:

> It just didn't feel like me; the whole situation felt so outlandish ... And because Jonny [Epstein, who played Shylock] is such a powerful presence, you're not going to get anything by him as an actor on stage or in rehearsal ... I felt all of this. I just tried to wrap it into the scene. The level of intimidation was high. I never got comfortable with the scene, and had a real experience of the clip at which the thought happens in Shakespeare ... And I just couldn't give myself more time because that wouldn't have been serving the text. I remember never feeling like I got that scene, always feeling behind, slightly behind, that my mind was not shifting fast enough, because Shakespeare's writing takes these leaps. I felt disembodied, and I kept putting that into the scene ... Portia's no dummy, and she's studied a lot ... But she's never done this before. (2021; Figure 8).

FIGURE 8 *Guard (Thomas Brazzle), Antonio (John Hadden), Portia (Tamara Hickey) and Shylock (Jonathan Epstein). Photo: Ava G. Lindenmaier. Reproduced with the permission of Ava G. Lindenmaier.*

Hickey acknowledged that despite her discomfort audiences 'responded really well to that scene and it always surprised me, because as an actor, I never felt that I was in control of my vehicle' (2021). Some actors and directors might see what happened to Hickey as a shortcoming or flaw in the process. However, in my view, this is precisely the strength of Packer's approach. If Hickey were really out of control in the scene, she would have lost her composure and failed to maintain the performance, which is known in acting parlance as 'breaking character'. Instead, because she is both technically skilled in the structure of the verse as well as emotionally available to the language, the structure of the verse held her even as she felt as if she were ready to veer out of control moment by moment. Hickey was inhabiting the language of the text as her experience and that experience resonated with the audience. Hickey's experience of the courtroom became Portia's experience and

Portia's was Hickey's. She was working on the edge and that is a measure of her emotional courage and technical skill.

While the courtroom scene challenged Hickey's Portia, Epstein's Shylock once again endured the 'Mad Scene' on his way to the courtroom. Both moments were painful to witness. As Packer explained:

> We used the same device in those horrid scenes where Salerio and Salario are baiting Shylock. Jonny entered, holding the dress to him as he was grieving the loss of his daughter, Jessica. They wrenched it away and tossed it around like a ball, and he was frantic trying to get it back. In the 1998 production you had the feeling that if Jonny got hold of that dress, he would have kicked them to bits, whereas in the 2016 you could see the cost to him because he was nearly two decades older and his body showed Shylock's suffering. You could see him hesitating. Both times it was bloody painful. Shakespeare doesn't back away from the cruelty and racism in the play. He really doesn't. (2021a)

The courtroom scene was also different for Epstein, particularly Shylock's monologue that begins, 'What judgment should I dread, doing no wrong? / You have among you many a purchased slave' (4.1.89–93). Epstein explained,

> The sense of violence of the Holocaust was much more immediate in '98, and so I was angry on behalf of my victimhood, whereas in 2016, I was angrier on behalf of all victims. My outrage was a more universal outrage, an outrage against hypocrisy rather than brutality. (2021)

The universal outrage of Epstein's Shylock rippled through the 2016 production, revealing how much had changed in America over the past two decades. The seemingly irreconcilable political divisions in the country were becoming painfully clear, and, with the growth of the 'Me, too' and 'Black Lives

Matter' movements, America's history of racism and sexism could no longer be ignored.

Packer's 2016 production grappled with these issues in the portrayal of the enslaved as veiled women. Moreover, one of the Sals going after Shylock was played with courage by Cloteal Horne. Horne, who is a Black woman, brought a new dimension to the baiting of Shylock. The scene that emerged between Thomas Brazzle's Launcelot Gobbo and Deaon Griffin-Pressley's Lorenzo brought a new dimension to the play.

Launcelot Gobbo and Lorenzo

'We found something in terms of this side character that is often just there to be the clown.'

(BRAZZLE 2022)

On the first day of scene rehearsals following *dropping in* Deaon Griffin-Pressley, who played Lorenzo, and Thomas Brazzle, who played Launcelot Gobbo, 'just started riffing on their first scene' (Brazzle 2022), 3.5, in which Lorenzo asserts his status over Launcelot while Launcelot uses comic misprision to eschew obedience. The freedom of the process encouraged them to follow their impulses as they engaged with the text, and they quickly realized that their competition in front of Jessica had taken a turn. Theirs was not a scene about an aspiring man of the middling sort trying to establish his authority over a house servant and the play's clown. Instead, what emerged was a conflict between two Black Americans exploring the weight of their history.[8]

Raphael Massie, the associate director with them in the rehearsal room, described the result as 'one of the most brilliant choices that I had ever seen; as two Black men challenging each other in terms of status, it made perfect sense as to how that conversation could go' (2022).

In the play Lorenzo is higher in status than Launcelot Gobbo, yet the difference is unclear. In their move to Belmont both end up serving Portia and Bassanio, albeit in different capacities. Portia makes Lorenzo the steward of her household in her absence while Launcelot has left Shylock to become Bassanio's man. In scene 3.5, they go back and forth, each upping the ante until Lorenzo uses his position to dismiss Launcelot, who is supposed to exit. But on that first day of rehearsal Brazzle didn't leave: 'for some reason I still don't know why, I decided, I'm not exiting. I stood there and stared him down' (2022).

The competition began when Griffin-Pressley's Lorenzo entered at 3.5.19 to discover Kate Abbruzzese's Jessica and Brazzle's Launcelot engaged in a repartee over the state of her soul as a Jewish woman marrying a Christian. Upon seeing their *téte-a-téte*, Lorenzo quipped, 'I shall grow jealous of you shortly, Launcelot, if you thus get my wife into corners'. The witty quip suggests some anxiety on Lorenzo's part. Jessica and Launcelot Gobbo have known each other much longer, and Launcelot was also their go-between. During *dropping in*, Brazzle found that his Launcelot was in love with Jessica, and that there was more to his character's story than simply serving as the comic relief in the play:

> When I first read the part, I thought 'this character's pretty funny' and my next thought was that Tina is going to want to go deeper ... Tina had given us a prompt before the first day of rehearsal, asking us to think about identity and what it means to belong ... I started to think about my personal truth as an African American and about how Launcelot Gobbo was a servant who wanted to break away, but at the same time was in love with this woman that society wasn't going to let him be with. What I loved about the casting was that Lorenzo was also played by a Black actor, but was higher in class. During the rehearsal process, I started to feel like our dynamic was similar to the divisions between upper echelon Black people and the rest of us. (Brazzle 2022)

For his part Deaon Griffin-Pressley felt the need to differentiate Lorenzo from Launcelot, especially in front of his 'white identifying wife' whom he wanted to impress: 'There was no way Lorenzo was going to be flamboyant like Launcelot Gobbo – the joker, the clown – no way. I felt my higher status as Lorenzo only came from marrying Jessica – other than that I was the same as Launcelot – so I started demeaning him and treating him like he was an enslaved person' (Griffin-Pressley 2021). The actors picked up the suggestion in the text of a rivalry between Launcelot Gobbo and Lorenzo over Jessica when Abbruzzese's Jessica playfully replied that he needn't worry because they (she and Launcelot) are 'out', since Launcelot has told her she will have no mercy as a Jew's daughter and that Lorenzo is 'no good member of the commonwealth' because 'in converting Jews to Christians he raise[s] the price of pork' (3.5.24–26). Hearing this, Griffin-Pressley's Lorenzo turned on Brazzle's Launcelot, retorting that he 'shall answer that better to the commonwealth than you can the getting up of the Negro's belly. The Moor is with child by you, Launcelot' (3.5.28–29). Packer prepared the audience to notice this detail by adding a brief dumb show earlier in the production, just before Brazzle's Launcelot Gobbo left Shylock's employment. In the dumb show Launcelot Gobbo encountered the 'Moor', played by Cloteal Horne, costumed as an enslaved woman, who teased him with a carrot. He chased her around and then offstage. Brazzle's Launcelot couldn't believe that Lorenzo exposed him in the presence of Jessica. He thought, 'this dude just outed me – like you don't do that, man, you know what's up' (Brazzle 2022). In the discussion that followed, both Brazzle and Griffin-Pressley agreed that this moment started a spiral causing them to break 'Black codes' (Griffin-Pressley 2021). Theirs was now a struggle that went deeper than status. Griffin-Pressley's Lorenzo turned to Jessica and, as the text indicates, mocked Launcelot as he stood there: 'How every fool can play upon the word! I think the best grace of wit will shortly turn into silence, and discourse grow commendable in none only but parrots' (3.5.33–35). He then ordered Launcelot to leave (3.5.35). Brazzle's Launcelot made it clear he was 'giving him the finger' (2021) when he responded: 'For the table, *sir*, it shall be served in; for the meat, *sir*, it shall be covered; for your coming in to dinner, *sir*, why let it be, as humors and conceits shall govern' (3.5.46–48). He refused to exit, daring Lorenzo to mock him again to his face. After a beat, Griffin-Pressley realized what Brazzle was up to, and decided, 'Screw it, I'm just going to do this speech right in front of you' (Griffin-Pressley 2021). He turned to Jessica and spoke his lines 'in such a way that it was clear that Launcelot is one of those Blacks that he despises for being a goof and a clown' (Griffin-Pressley 2021): 'O dear discretion, how his words are suited! / … / A many fools, that stand in better place, / Garnished like him, that for a tricksy word / Defy the matter' (3.5.46-8). Brazzle's Launcelot knew Lorenzo was 'using the speech to break me down and get me out of there. I looked over to Jessica. She didn't say anything. That's when I thought, "Yep, I am what they say I am"' (Brazzle 2022).

In response to Jessica's silence, Brazzle's Gobbo upped the ante at the next rehearsal when they worked the play's final scene. At the top of the scene Lorenzo and Jessica were alone in the garden on a night in which, as Griffin-Pressley's Lorenzo remarked, the 'moon shines bright' (5.1.1), indicating that there was sufficient light to see and recognize people. Brazzle's Launcelot entered to announce that Bassanio would arrive in the morning, pretending that he couldn't see Lorenzo. He called repeatedly for 'Master Lorenzo'; Lorenzo repeatedly answered, 'Here!' Launcelot repeatedly asked, 'Where?' Lorenzo, replied with increasing frustration, 'Here'. Brazzle's Launcelot refused to acknowledge Griffin-Pressley's Lorenzo for the entire scene. After calling and searching, he stood directly in front of Lorenzo pretending he didn't recognize him (or his voice) in order to flout him one last time: 'Tell [Lorenzo] my master will be here ere morning' (5.1.45.46). As he said these, Launcelot's final words in the play, Brazzle 'let a little slip' of what he calls 'the "step n'fetch" Sambo Blackface thing' to say "This is how you see me. This is what you want me to be"' (2021).

Brazzle's 'soft shoe shuffle' (Massie 2022) led to the next escalation. When they returned to rehearse scene 3.5, they realized that Lorenzo treats Launcelot like an enslaved person on the auction block. As Griffin-Pressley recalled, the suggestion 'came out of the text' (Griffin-Pressley 2021) in the way Lorenzo puts Launcelot on display, demeaning and dehumanizing him in front of everyone, not only Jessica, but the theatre audience as well: 'It was one of the deepest experiences I remember having with Shakespeare' (Griffin-Pressley 2021). While speaking Lorenzo's lines (3.5.46–8), Griffin-Pressley used his gestures to enact the point: 'he took off Launcelot's shirt. He pulled out his arms to show how strong he was. He slapped him on the chest to show that this "slave" was durable and sturdy and would be a good worker' (Massie 2022). As Massie explained:

> Gobbo is limited in what tactics he is able to use because Lorenzo has the higher status. And so they go back and forth. But at the end of the day, Lorenzo comes out on top because Gobbo can only do so much. So this idea of an enslaved Black man and a free Black man within the frame of the auction block strips away everything and goes straight for the heart. And that was the microcosm of the production. (Massie 2022)

When Brazzle, Griffin-Pressley and Massie approached Packer with what they discovered, she was astounded and encouraged them to keep working on the scene. Their emotional availability in confronting the text, finding in it a conflict that spoke to their own experience, affording them a means to explore, acknowledge and reveal themselves to the audience in it, fulfilled her long-standing conviction that multicultural casting is the only way to realize fully the complex dimensions of Shakespeare's plays.

Raphael Massie felt that having a diverse artistic cast and crew was a key factor in creating a safe space for the actors to explore:

> The diversity of the cast and the creative team overall was essential in even being able to generate a story like that scene. And it all started with a willingness from everyone involved to say, okay, we're coming into this play which can and has caused a lot of harm. How can we speak from our own lived experiences and come together to tell a unified and cohesive story, one that's going to make people uncomfortable, but hopefully start a dialogue going forward. (2022)

As in the 1998 production, Packer placed Shylock's singing of the Kol Nidre just prior to the play's comic resolution with the rings. Shylock was offstage. As in 1998, the audience could hear but not see him. Once again, the Kol Nidre could not be contained by the play's comic ending, which, for Tamara Hickey did not feel particularly comic in any case. She struggled to follow the language of the text and move past what she had experienced in the courtroom scene: 'There was so much subtext in that scene for me' (2021). She had picked up on the energy between Hadden's Antonio and Isaac's Bassanio 'in secrecy, in disguise, and then for it to end the way it does … it's a big leap to make' (2021). While understanding that 'there's room for complexity, there's room for all of it', she was 'trying not to play it because it's all supposed to be in the language. But the language felt really unsatisfying for me, and a little disjointed and disconnected because of what had come before. It felt tragic' (2021). It makes sense to me that Hickey's Portia felt that way, because she found that complexity in herself and allowed it to be alive in her body every night of the performance. Her Portia would not be the first person to have mixed emotions after marrying someone. Shakespeare's plays tread a precarious line between comedy and tragedy, a line that Frances Dolan aptly describes as 'fine' and 'unstable' (1999: xxxi).

Daniel Levy's arrangement of Monteverdi's 'Damigella tutta bela' inserted a jolt of uplift and release as the cast came together to dance. Yet what lingered was Jonathan Epstein chanting the Kol Nidre, this time indicating a universal message: 'Shylock's voice dominates the encroaching darkness as Jessica stands, isolated in fading light, listening. The cost, not just of doing business but of living itself, is indeed high' (Borak 2016: D3).

It has been over half a century since Clive Barnes 'wonder[ed] whether, with all its racist overtones, *The Merchant of Venice* has not taken [*King Lear's*] place as Shakespeare's unstageable play' (1970). Packer's two productions of the play, in 1998 and 2016 indicate that, far from being unstageable, it is, perhaps, the play that speaks most poignantly to the complexities of America's interwoven racial, religious, political and cultural issues.

Epilogue

The Kol Nidre, which means 'All Vows', is often described as a legal formula. It is nevertheless a formula that embraces an expansive view of the human condition. The Kol Nidre, the opening prayer of Yom Kippur, prepares for the personal mending of sin. As a chant oriented towards the future, it asks that all personal vows that have been made or might be made in error over the coming year be annulled. The metaphysical view of the Kol Nidre is one that embraces the potential for transformation, for breaking free, even from a vow. It is a perspective in which people are not defined by their mistakes but are granted the opportunity to remake themselves, to begin anew, so as not be 'lost in a repeating cycle of regret' (Gelber 2020). In this way it reaches not only into the 'depths of the self, but also into the fabric of reality' (Gelber 2020).[9] The Kol Nidre is premised upon the power and authenticity of the words we speak, words with which we begin and begin again, words through which we 'make [our] appearance in the human world' (Arendt 1998: 179).

Tina Packer's original method of directing, *dropping in*, similarly honours the power of words, focussing on the energy and creativity of the actors, inviting each of them to forge a profound, dynamic connection with Shakespeare's text, with each other and with the audience. Actors and directors struggle to find ways to make Shakespeare current and new, to break through the weight of history, of a past haunted by performances both tedious and brilliant. Packer's *dropping in* is a process that by its nature produces original work. Her approach to directing embraces past and present, manifesting her conviction that the function of theatre is to explore difficult questions, helping us to understand one another and thereby heal – one word at a time.

Packer closed her fourth decade performing as well as directing. In the spring of 2017, Packer played Volumnia in Lantern Theater's *Coriolanus*. The reviewer for *The Philadelphia Inquirer* wrote, 'the evening belonged to Tina Packer, utterly mesmerizing as Volumnia. A stage mother from hell, she's alternately seductive, cloying, vicious, and servile in her attempts to manipulate her son. Packer makes us believe she could single-handedly rule Rome' (Derakhshani 2017). Her *Cymbeline* that summer at Shakespeare & Company was performed in the round, bare bard style with a cast of nine playing multiple roles.[10] Packer cast Thomas Brazzle as Posthumous, the romantic lead, if you will, and Deaon Griffin-Pressley as Pisanio, the servant, thereby reversing their respective status in the roles they played the previous year in *Merchant*. As the world tentatively emerged from the Covid pandemic in the summer of 2021, Packer, now in her fifth decade of directing, greeted audiences with her staging of Debra Ann Byrd's one woman show, *Becoming Othello*, which opened at Shakespeare & Company's Roman Garden Theatre. One reviewer wrote that Debra Ann Byrd 'moves from the lyrical to the dramatic to the rapturous on this "Black Girl's Journey," guided by her own fine instincts and Packer's critical eye' (Bergman 2021). Packer followed this success with an 'electric' and 'very funny' (Garver 2022: 10) production of *Titus Andronicus* in the round at the Portland Playhouse in Portland, Oregon. This brings us full circle to her 2023 production of *Henry VI Part II* where we began.

Conclusion

When Packer founded her company in 1978, the regional Shakespeare theatre movement in America was just gaining momentum on the heels of the mid-century regional theatre movement. By the early 1990s there were Shakespeare Theatres in every state, while 1991 saw the founding of the Shakespeare Theatre Association of America, whose mission was 'To provide a forum for the artistic, managerial, and educational leadership for theatres primarily involved with the production of the works of William Shakespeare; to discuss issues and methods of work, to share resources, and information; and to act as an advocate for Shakespearean productions and training' (http://www.stahome.org/). The organization changed its name in 2011 to The Shakespeare Theatre Association in order to reflect its international membership. The founding of this organization is perhaps the most tangible sign that, by the end of the twentieth century, Americans were feeling at home in Shakespeare's plays.

Tina Packer's approach to Shakespeare played a significant role in this development. She never strove to become an auteur director with instant name recognition. Rather her focus was on her work with each individual actor, helping them to make Shakespeare's language their own. Her influence spread steadily over the years through the work of her company and the success of her productions. Within a few years of the founding of the company, Shakespeare & Company was known as a place to train and perform for actors and artistic staff who were serious about their craft. Word spread, not only in the many newspaper articles about the company but also through those who work in the theatre, and the hundreds, perhaps thousands of actors, directors, movement and fight choreographers who were trained and continue to train at Shakespeare & Company. Many have gone on to found their own companies, take positions as faculty in theatre departments and succeed as actors on stage and screen. Today Tina Packer is considered one of the most distinguished directors of Shakespeare in America.[11]

Packer's story is both exemplary of and singular within a historical perspective of Shakespearean theatre in America. It is singular because she herself is a remarkable woman of vision and boundless energy. An exceptionally talented actor herself, she is an empathetic director with a unique method of allowing actors to feel open and free in expressing themselves during rehearsal while she guides their collective energy towards a cohesive work of art. Her story is exemplary because it illuminates the importance of regional Shakespeare across the United States. These regional theatres play vital roles in local communities, teaching in school programs, organizing theatre and therapy workshops for veterans, working with prison populations and helping troubled youth. They encourage diversity through their training and casting as well as their programming, emphasizing contemporary playwrights of colour and women alongside the plays of Shakespeare. Indeed, as Martha LoMonaco writes, 'American regional theatre has become *the* national theatre, collectively representing all areas of the country (including New York City) with its diversity of race, ethnicity, religion and cultural heritage' (2006: 246). For Packer, it all began with a question, and she has never stopped asking questions, inviting her actors to discover themselves so that her audience may do so as well.

APPENDIX

Productions directed by Tina Packer

* *London Academy of Music and Dramatic Art*
** State University of New York
*** Plays co-directed by Tina Packer

Year	Play	Author	Venue or Location
1971–73	Measure for Measure	Shakespeare	LAMDA*
	The Winter's Tale	Shakespeare	LAMDA
	Hamlet	Shakespeare	LAMDA
	Twelfth Night	Shakespeare	LAMDA
	King Lear	Shakespeare	LAMDA
	The Seagull	Anton Chekov	LAMDA
	Erpingham Camp	Joe Orton	LAMDA
	The Storm	Aleksandr Ostrovsky	LAMDA
	Ghost Sonata	August Strindberg	LAMDA
	The Rivals	Richard Sheridan	LAMDA

Year	Play	Author	Venue or Location
1974	*The Taming of the Shrew*	Shakespeare	The Performing Garage, NYC
	The Winter's Tale	Shakespeare	O'Neill Theatre, CT
1975	*King Lear*	Shakespeare	Riverside Studios, London
1977	*Richard III*	Shakespeare	NYU Tisch School of the Arts
	Henry VI Parts 1, 2, &3	Shakespeare	NYU Tisch School of the Arts
	The Learned Ladies	Moliere/ Richard Wilbur	Smith College
	Romeo and Juliet	Shakespeare	SUNY** Purchase
1978	*The Learned Ladies*	Moliere/ Richard Wilbur	Kennedy Center
	A Midsummer Night's Dream	Shakespeare	The Mount Mainstage
1979	*The Winter's Tale*	Shakespeare	The Mount Mainstage
	Romeo and Juliet	Shakespeare	The Mount Mainstage
1980	*The Tempest*	Shakespeare	The Mount Mainstage

Year	**Play**	**Author**	**Venue or Location**
1981	*Twelfth Night*	Shakespeare	The Mount Mainstage
	As You Like It	Shakespeare	The Mount Mainstage
1982	*Macbeth*	Shakespeare	The Mount Mainstage
	Twelfth Night	Shakespeare	The Mount Mainstage
1983	*The Comedy of Errors*	Shakespeare	The Mount Mainstage
1984	*A Midsummer Night's Dream****	Shakespeare	The Mount Mainstage
	Romeo and Juliet***	Shakespeare	The Mount Mainstage
1985	*The Comedy of Errors*	Shakespeare	The Mount Mainstage
1986	*Rat in the Skull*	Ron Hutchinson	Boston Shakespeare Company
	Anthony and Cleopatra	Shakespeare	The Mount Mainstage
	Master Harold and the Boys	Athol Fugard	Boston Shakespeare Company

Year	Play	Author	Venue or Location
1987	*Observe the Sons of Ulster Marching Towards the Somme*	Frank McGuinness	Boston Shakespeare Company
1988	*As You Like It*	Shakespeare	The Mount Mainstage
1989	*The Tempest*	Shakespeare	The Mount Mainstage
	Roman Fever	Edith Wharton	The Mount Salon
1990	*As You Like It*	Shakespeare	The Mount Mainstage
	Roman Fever	Edith Wharton	The Mount Salon
1991	*Hamlet*	Shakespeare	North Shore Music Theatre
	Othello	Shakespeare	New York Theatre Inst., NY
1992	*A Life in the Theatre*	David Mamet	The Stables
	Duet for One	Tom Kempinski	The Stables
	Julius Caesar	Shakespeare	The Stables

Year	Play	Author	Venue or Location
1993	*Julius Caesar*	Shakespeare	The Stables
	Duet for One	Tom Kempinski	The Stables
	Midsummer Night's Dream	Shakespeare	The Mount Mainstage
	Scheherazade	Marisha Chamberlain	Canadian Stage Co., Toronto
	Duet for One	Tom Kempinski	Boston Center for the Arts
	*Berkeley Square***	J.L. Balderston	Boston Center for the Arts
1994	*Mrs. Klein*	Nicholas Wright	The Stables
1995	*Much Ado About Nothing*	Shakespeare	The Mount Mainstage
1996	*Merry Wives of Windsor*	Shakespeare	The Mount Mainstage
	Measure for Measure	Shakespeare	The Mount Mainstage

Year	Play	Author	Venue or Location
1997	*The Death of the Father of Psychoanalysis (& Anna)*	Bridget Carpenter	The Stables
	Henry IV, Part 1***	Shakespeare	The Mount Mainstage
	Measure for Measure (all female)	Shakespeare	L.A. Women's Shakespeare Festival
1998	*The Merchant of Venice*	Shakespeare	The Mount Mainstage
	The Millionairess	George Bernard Shaw	The Stables
1999	*Richard III*	Shakespeare	Duffin Theatre
	Summer	Edith Wharton	The Stables
	Richard III	Shakespeare	Harvard/Radcliffe
2000	*Coriolanus*	Shakespeare	The Stables
2001	*Coriolanus*	Shakespeare	Founders' Theatre
	A Midsummer Night's Dream	Shakespeare	The Mount Mainstage

Year	Play	Author	Venue or Location
2002	*Macbeth*	Shakespeare	Founders' Theatre
	The Scarlet Letter	Carol Gilligan	Founders' Theatre
2003	*King Lear*	Shakespeare	Founders' Theatre
	The Fly-Bottle	David Egan	Spring Lawn
2004	*The Othello Project*	Shakespeare	Founders' Theatre
2005	*King John*	Shakespeare	Founders' Theatre
	Ice Glen	Joan Ackermann	Spring Lawn
	The Tell-Tale Poe	Edgar Allan Poe	Founders' Theatre
2007	*Coriolanus*	Shakespeare	Mercury Theatre, Colchester, England
2008	*All's Well That Ends Well*	Shakespeare	Founders' Theatre
	The Lear Project	Shakespeare	Elayne Bernstein Theatre

Year	Play	Author	Venue or Location
2010	*The Taster*	Joan Ackermann	Founders' Theatre
	Pericles	Shakespeare	American Shakespeare Center
2011	*The Learned Ladies*	Moliere/ Richard Wilbur	Elayne Bernstein Theatre
2012	*Richard III*	Shakespeare	Colorado Shakespeare Festival
	Troilus & Cressida	Shakespeare	Actors' Shakespeare Project
2013	*Henry VIII*	Shakespeare	Actors' Shakespeare Project
2014	*Julius Caesar*	Shakespeare	Prague Shakespeare Theatre
			Orlando Shakespeare Theatre
2016	*The Merchant of Venice*	Shakespeare	Tina Packer Playhouse
	Henry VI, part 2	Shakespeare	Actors' Shakespeare Project

Year	Play	Author	Venue or Location
2017	*Cymbeline*	Shakespeare	Tina Packer Playhouse
2018	*Heisenberg*	Simon Stephens	Tina Packer Playhouse
2019	*The Waverly Gallery*	Kenneth Lonergan	Elayne Bernstein Theatre
2021	*Becoming Othello*	Debra Ann Byrd	Roman Garden Theatre
2022	*Titus Andronicus*	Shakespeare	Portland Playhouse
2023	*Henry VI Part 2*	Shakespeare	Tina Packer Playhouse

NOTES

Preface

1 Packer has promulgated her message not only as a director but also as the author of several books, including: *Shakespeare & Company When Action is Eloquence*, co-authored with Bella Merlin, New York: Routledge (2020); *Women of Will: The Remarkable Evolution of Shakespeare's Female Characters*, Vintage Paperbacks (2016); *Tales from Shakespeare: Shakespeare's stories for children*, Scholastic (2004); *Power Plays: Shakespeare's Lessons in Leadership and Management*, co-authored with Columbia Business School professor John O. Whitney, Simon & Schuster (2001).

Introduction

1 I italicize Packer's original practice, *dropping in*, in order to align it with the way it is referred to in Merlin and Packer (2020).

2 Packer's process gives the actor agency over the development of the character's identity. From the beginning she has incorporated check-ins before, after, and during rehearsal as necessary to talk about the emotions that emerge. Packer builds the world of her productions out of the actors' creativity and emotional topography, an openness that has been central from the beginning. It therefore seems that her approach has, of its nature, addressed the concerns raised in Ayanna Thompson's essay, 'Practicing a Theory/Theorizing a Practice', *Colorblind Shakespeare* (2006: 1–24). Thompson elaborates on Elin Diamond's point regarding the 'violent nature of mimesis', particularly when 'actors of color' are 'asked to perform roles

and perhaps incorporate what is potentially the "rivalrous other" (14). Thompson points out that all multicultural productions (not only 'colorblind' ones) should make time for 'painful discussions about identity' because the 'mimetic nature of performance destabilizes identity' (14).

3 The word 'presence' here denotes the change in the physical presence of the actor. It is not referring to the theoretical debate over presence in live theatre versus film and other modalities. For a discussion of that question, see Power (2008).

4 When Packer was with the Royal Shakespeare Company (RSC), she learned structure of the verse from John Barton. She also learned from him that the flow and structure of the scenes are indicated in the text, and she encourages the actors to find that flow.

5 For further reading on Packer's process, particularly how it developed, see Merlin and Packer (2020: 7–61).

6 In the early years of the company when there was no email and everyone was rehearsing and living at The Mount, Packer would gather her actors together to give them her questions sometime before the start of rehearsal.

7 I spoke with several of Packer's composers and sound designers and all of them remarked on how appreciative and respectful Packer was of their work and the care and attention that she gave the music and sound cues during the technical rehearsal with the cast.

8 Except where I cite Packer and Linklater directly, this summary of how Packer came to found Shakespeare & Company with Kristin Linklater and Dennis Krausnick is indebted to Merlin and Packer (2020: 9–35).

9 Packer's application was supported by letters of recommendation from Peter Hall and Trevor Nunn, who knew her from her time as an actor at the Royal Shakespeare Company.

10 Dennis Krausnick and Tina Packer were together as a couple from the time of the founding of the company and eventually married.

11 Coe, Richard L. (1978).

12 The area is now known as Theatre Row.
13 This information is from documents in the Shakespeare & Company archives and was also reported in several newspapers at the time.
14 Shakespeare & Company chose to leave The Mount three years before the lease expired in 2004.
15 https://shakespeare.org/our-theaters/
16 Elayne Bernstein and her family led a multimillion-dollar campaign for the construction of the building named for her and Arthur Waldstein was a major contributor to the outdoor amphitheatre named for him.
17 For the evolution of the company's structure, see Merlin and Packer (2020: 38–60). For the company's current structure, see the website: https://www.shakespeare.org/meet-the-team.
18 I am indebted to Jonathan Epstein, who coined the phrase 'grand mise en scène' to describe the style of Packer's outdoor productions.
19 With the exception of *The Merchant of Venice* and *Twelfth Night,* all citations of Shakespeare's plays are from *The Norton Shakespeare*, ed. S. Greenblatt,. New York: Norton, 2008, Citations for *The Merchant of Venice* are from Kaplan 2002, Citations for *Twelfth Night* are from Warren and Wells 1998.

Chapter 1

1 This chapter heading is quoted from: Eugene O'Neill, *Long Days Journey into Night*, New Haven and London: Yale University Press 1968: 150.
2 The Five College Consortium is a higher education non-profit organization that includes the following colleges in the Northeast: Amherst, Hampshire, Mount Holyoke, Smith and the University of Massachusetts (https://www.fivecolleges.edu/).
3 Morton and Packer met at the symposium on classical theatre at The Mount in 1978 and wanted to work together. Morton played Caliban the year before in Gerald Freedman's production at the Stratford Festival in Connecticut. Presumably Morton liked the character and wanted to play Caliban again in a

different context. Morton was the only Black actor in Freeman's production, which embodied the trope that Caliban represented Prospero's libido while Ariel represented the 'the best aspects of the artist' (Saccio 1980). See Errol Hill (1984).

4 Packer's *Tempest* resembled Jonathan Miller's 1971 production at the RSC, with an important difference. While Miller's version had Ariel subjugate Caliban at the end of the play, in Packer's production it was a Stephano, the butler, who tried and failed to subjugate Caliban.

5 I can only surmise that reviewers wrongly assumed that the production was meant to be colourblind, as none of them mentioned whether any of the actors were white or Black, including Joe Morton.

6 This idea is from my experience of clown training led by Dave Demke and Jane Nichols at Shakespeare & Company.

7 This idea is from my experience of clown training with Michael Toomey at Shakespeare & Company.

8 Rocco Sisto played Malvolio in that production as well.

Chapter 2

1 This chapter heading is quoted from: Edith Wharton, *The Age of Innocence,* New York: Barnes and Noble Classics 2004: 146.

2 Packer played the role earlier at Gloucester stage and at Shakespeare & Company. This performance was notable as it was her first time performing in one of Boston's theatres.

3 The 1993 production followed the same staging with a change in one actor: Malcolm Ingram replaced James Goodwin Rice as Julius Caesar, Messala and Lepidus.

4 The production travelled to Foxboro, Massachusetts near Boston in September. The staging remained the same. This review is from the Foxboro performance.

5 The production files contained images and sketches, which helped me visualize the set. I am grateful to Steve Ball, company manager, for giving me access to the files.

# Chapter 3

1 This chapter heading is quoted from: *A Midsummer Night's Dream*, 2.2.153
2 Shakespeare & Company's non-equity actors frequently perform in the summer at 'The Dell', a small outdoor theatre at The Mount.
3 In clown training and performance at Shakespeare & Company, 'the drop' refers to the clown's moment of humiliation.
4 The word 'spirit' appears three times, in the play, while 'spirits' occurs five times. These instances range in meaning from the 'spirits' accompanying Hecate (3.5.34–74), Ross's description of Macbeth 'curbing [Cawdor's] wild spirit' (1.2.57), to Macbeth's encounter with the apparitions when the last is 'too like the spirit of Banquo' whose 'crown does sear [his] eyeballs' (4.1.128–9). Hecate's magic distills a 'vap'rous drop' from the 'corner of the moon to 'raise such artificial sprites / As by the strength of their illusion / Shall draw [Macbeth] on to his confusion' (3.5.23–28). Lady Macbeth, in turn, plans to 'pour [her] spirits in [Macbeth's] ear' (1.5.24) and, as she learns of his arrival, conjures the 'spirits' that will guide her 'fell purpose' (1.2.38–44), the 'spirits' that 'shine through' the murderers Macbeth hires to kill Banquo (3.1.129) and 'The spirits that' Macbeth believes, 'know / All mortal consequences' (5.3.3–4).
5 As Stephen Greenblatt observes, 'the witches [dance] around the caldron, and, the play seems to imply, the caldron is in every one of us' (2008b).
6 The play can indeed be relentless, particularly in the intimate space of the playhouse. I've been to productions of *Macbeth* where I experienced claustrophobia. The effects of the play's language and imagery on the psyche accumulate.
7 As Greenblatt puts it, *King Lear* explores the 'awful silence of the gods' and raises the possibility that this silence, 'may equally be a sign of their indifference or their nonexistence' (Greenblatt 2008c: 2326). *Macbeth* places us in inbetweeness as well: on the one hand it 'invite[s] us to recoil' from 'Macbeth's vision of life' while on the other hand it invites us to 'recoil from too confident and simple a celebration of the triumph of grace' (Greenblatt 2008b: 2576-7). The ambivalence of *King John*, as Walter Cohen

writes, is 'the uncertain relationship between intention and outcome in a world that offers only fragments of an overarching consolation – religious or otherwise – for the frequent futility of human endeavour' (Cohen 2008: 1045).

8 Eleanor's retort to Constance, 'Thy bastard shall be king / that thou mayst be a queen and check the world' (2.1.121–123), uses the metaphor of chess. Arthur's capture and ensuing death, following hard upon his mother's suggests that Shakespeare was current on the latest changes in chess, which, as William Poole points out, had recently made the queen the most powerful piece on the board. Arthur's death recalls Nicholas Breton's poem 'The Chesse-Play', which concludes, 'Loose not the Queene, for ten to one, / If she be lost, the game is gone' (cited in Poole 2004: 55).

9 Prior to his key scenes in act 4, Arthur speaks a total of eight lines in five scenes. These few lines nevertheless reveal his character and prepare for the brave, eloquent child of act 4 that is the heart of the play.

10 For a searching response to Packer's Cleopatra, see Yu Jin Ko (2008: 161–74).

Chapter 4

1 Tony Simotes, the company's fight master (trained by B. H. Barry), who played Puck in the company's inaugural production, served as artistic director from 2009–16. He was succeeded in 2017 by Allyn Burrows, another long-standing company member, who is the present artistic director.

2 https://cupresents.org/performance/10376/shakespeare/richard-iii/

3 See Introduction.

4 Similar arguments have been made by literary critics: Gaber (2004); Edward (2002). I am indebted to Stephen Purcell for these references.

5 Some believe that in medieval and early modern Europe when Jews were forced to convert, it allowed them to do so in order to survive without giving up their faith. Chanting the prayer would

abnegate the conversion, so they could continue to worship in secret. This has a special resonance for Shakespeare's time, when, after the Reformation in England, Catholics as well Jews were faced with forced conversions and practicing their faith covertly. The history of the Kol Nidre is extraordinarily complex. For the most recent scholarship on the topic see Moshe Benovitz's open access book: *Kol Nidre: Studies in the Development of Rabbinic Votive Institutions*. Brown Judaic Studies, 2020. https://doi.org/10.2307/j.ctvzpv5pq. On Shakespeare's audience, M. Lindsay Kaplan writes: 'While the play clearly draws on a tradition of theological conflict between Christians and Jews, it also reflects issues of contemporary concern within Christianity' (242). For an analysis of how Shakespeare's original audience may have identified with Shylock, see her edition of the play, especially, 242–59.

6 Levy noted, 'the time and care [Packer] took with the original scores, making sure the music was serving the story, adding a rehearsal just to teach the actors how to hear and work with the music cues. That is rare in a director, and had a bracing effect on our production' (Levy email 6 March 2023).

7 For these descriptions of the rehearsal exercises I am indebted to several cast members from the production: Bella Merlin, John Hadden, Shahar Isaac, Cloteal Horne, Thomas Brazzle and Deaon Griffin-Pressley.

8 Both actors referred to themselves in our interview as African Americans. I am using the adjective 'Black' because that is preferred in current usage, and I want to acknowledge that this is not how they referred to themselves. Griffin-Pressley, in particular, prefers not to be referred to as 'Black': 'I believe that my people are much more than the opposite of white … I ask people to call me golden or African American, because I acknowledge that this is native American land' (2021).

9 I am grateful to David Gelber, a former student, now a poet living in Israel, for sharing with me his view of the 'Kol Nidre'.

10 For a detailed case study of the rehearsal process for that production, see Merlin and Packer (2020), 'Chapter 15: *Cymbeline*, A Performance Case study' (274–95).

11 Among her many honours, Packer has received three lifetime achievement awards: 1. The Ellen Stewart Career Achievement

in Professional Theatre Award (2023): awarded by ATHE (American Theatre in Education) ; 2. The American Shakespeare Center's Burbage Award (2009); 3. The Elliott Norton Award for Lifetime Achievement (2001).

REFERENCES

Anderson, Susan Heller (1982), 'Shakespeare in the Park, This Time in Brooklyn', *New York Times*, 2 July: C15.
Arendt, Hanna ([1958] 1998), *The Human Condition*, Chicago: Chicago University Press.
artincontext (2022), 'The Creation of Adam' by Michelangelo – The God Touching Adam Fresco', 19 July. Available online https://artincontext.org/the-creation-of-adam-by-michelangelo (accessed 10 September 2022).
Aspenlieder, Elizabeth (2022), 'Interview', 20 December.
Aucoin, Dan (2013), 'The Shifting Terrain of Power in "Henry VIII"', *The Boston Globe*, 18 December: G3.
Ballou, Bill (2022), 'Interview', 4 February.
Barba, Eugenio (2005), 'Barba, Eugenio, and Nicola Savarese, *A Dictionary of Theatre Anthropology: The Secret Art of the Performer*, Taylor & Francis Group', *ProQuest Ebook Central*. Available online http://ebookcentral.proquest.com/lib/csicuny/detail.action?docID=668433. Created from csicuny on 23 July 2023 18:48:25: 52–3.
Barclay, Bill (2022), 'Interview', 18 November.
Barnes, Clive (1970), *The New York Times*, 10 June: 39.
Bass, Milton R. (1980), '"The Tempest" at The Mount', *Berkshire Eagle*, 31 July: 9.
Bass, Milton (2002), *North Adams Transcript*, 11 July: 48.
Bassi, Shaul (2016), 'Shylock in Venice: Staging Shakespeare in the Ghetto', *YouTube*, uploaded by UCTV, 11 May 2016. Available online www.youtube.com/watch?v=1UusEqY2g9w.
Berek, Peter (1982), 'Shakespeare in the Berkshires', *Shakespeare Quarterly*, 33 (2): 212–13.
Bergman, Peter J. (2021), '"Becoming Othello: A Black Girl's Journey" is a Trip You Should Take', 21 July.
The Berkshire Eagle (1981), 16 April: 11.
Bock, Ariel (2021), 'Interview', 9 November.

Borak, Jeffrey (1988), 'Karen Allen Shines', *The Berkshire Eagle*, 11 July: B10.
Borak, Jeffrey (1998), 'The Trouble with Shylock', *The Berkshire Eagle*, 31 July: D1.
Borak, Jeffrey (2002), 'Shakespeare & Company at 25', *The Berkshire Eagle*, 10 May: D2.
Borak, Jeffrey (2005), 'Pawns in a Game', *The Berkshire Eagle*, 6 August: Art.
Borak, Jeffrey (2007), *The Berkshire Eagle*, 9 August: D3.
Borak, Jeffrey (2016), *The Berkshire Eagle*, 16 July: D3.
Boston Globe (1995), 'Best of 1995', 31 December: 35.
Brantley, Ben (1993), 'In the Rarefied Air, Shakespeare Accessible to All', *New York Times*, 27 August: C2.
Brantley, Ben (1995), 'Critic's Notebook', *New York Times*, 1 August: C13.
Brantley, Ben (1996), 'Critic's Notebook, *New York Times*, 28 August: C11.
Brantley, Ben (2005), 'The Powers that be Play Chess with War', *New York Times*, 20 August: B7.
Brantely, Ben (2006), 'Excitable Dane', *New York Times*, 15 July: B7.
Brantley, Ben (2008), 'Farewell the Tranquil Mind', *New York Times*, 9 August: B11.
Brazzle, Thomas (2022), 'Interview', 25 January.
Brown, Pamela (1994), 'A Midsummer Night's Dream by Tina Packer', *Shakespeare Bulletin*, 12 (2): 11–12.
Burrows, Allyn (2021), 'Interview', 18 November.
Burrows, Allyn (2023), 'Email', 16 January.
Byrne, Terry (1996), 'Shakespeare & Co.'s Production Measures Up', *Boston Herald*, 19 September: Arts and Lifestyle, 1.
Byrne, Terry (1999), *Boston Herald*, 14 July: Arts and Lifestyle, 3.
Byrne, Terry (2001), *Boston Herald*, 14 August: Arts and Lifestyle, 4.
Byrne, Terry (2002), *Boston Herald*, 21 June: Arts and Lifestyle, 7.
Byrne, Terry (2003), 'Lear: A Conflagration of Ambition, Jealousy, Paranoia', *Boston Herald*, 7 August: The Edge S7.
C., R. (1981), 'On Stage 81, *Twelfth Night* Sounds Fine', *The Globe and Mail*, 21 May.
Carr, Jay (1986), 'Antony and Cleopatra Falls Short at The Mount', *The Boston Globe*, 19 July: 10.

Cartelli, Thomas, (1983), 'Review of Macbeth', *Theatre Journal*, 35 (2): 253–6.
Clay, Carolyn (1988), 'Review of "As You Like It"', *The Boston Phoenix*, 9.
Clayton, Thomas (1985), 'Shakespeare at the Guthrie: Twelfth Night', *Shakespeare Quarterly*, 36 (3): 353–9.
Coe, Richard L. (1978), 'Festival Firsts for American College Theater', *The Washington Post*, 8 March.
Coffin, David (2023), 'Interview', 9 January.
Cohen, Walter (2008), 'Introduction: *The Life and Death of King John*', in S. Greenblatt, W. Cohen, J. E. Howard and K. E. Maus (eds), *The Norton Shakespeare*, 1045–51, New York: Norton.
Coleman, Kevin (2022a), 'Interview', 13 January.
Coleman, Kevin (2022b), 'Interview', 14 January.
Cook, Amy (2020), *Shakespearean Futures: Casting the Bodies of Tomorrow on Shakespeare's Stages Today*, Cambridge: Cambridge University Press.
Crew, Bob (1981), 'Shakespeare Made Clear', *Toronto Star*, 20 May.
Derakhshani, Tirdad (2017), 'Tina Packer Mesmerizes in Lantern Theater's Dynamic, Arresting "Coriolanus"', 17 March. Friday. Available online advance-lexis com.csi.ezproxy.cuny.edu/api/d ocument?collection=news&id=urn:contentItem:5N3S-87Y1-DY JT-20F4-0000000&context=1516831 (accessed 29 August 2023).
Dibble, Susan (2021), 'Interview', 17 December.
Dibble, Susan (2022a), 'Email', 4 April.
Dibble, Susan (2022b), 'Email', 21 November.
Dolan, Frances (1999, rpr. 2018), 'Introduction', in *The Comedy of Errors*, xxix–xl, New York: Penguin Random House.
Douglas, Timothy (2022), 'Interview', 17 January.
Duckett, Richard (2008), 'Shakespeare is a Family Affair', *Worcester Telegram & Gazette*, G1.
Dunning, Jennifer (1982), '"Twelfth Night" Staged in Prospect Park', *New York Times*, 11 July: L40.
Eck, Michael (1995), 'Light Humor and Dark Drama', 21 July: D5.
Eck, Michael (1997), 'Shakespeare and Co, Stellar in "Henry IV"', *The Times Union*, 5 August: B7.
Eck, Michael (1998), *The Times Union*, 28 August: B7.
Eck, Michael (2002), *The Times Union*, 21 June: D4.
Eck, Michael (2005), 'Company does justice to epic "King John"', *The Times Union*, 1 August: C4.

Eckert, Thor, Jr. (1980), 'The Bard and Carpentry Make a Well-rounded Company', *The Christian Science Monitor*, 8 September: 11.

Edward, Berry (2002), 'Laughing at "Others"', in A. Leggatt (ed.), *The Cambridge Companion to Shakespearean Comedy*, 123–38, Cambridge: Cambridge University Press.

Engstrom, John (1982), 'Lenox Sees an Ambitious "Macbeth"', *The Boston Globe*, 6 August: 23.

Engstrom, John (1983), 'Shakespeare & Co.'s Dazzling "Comedy of Errors"', *The Boston Globe*, 22 August: 23.

Engstrom, John (1984), '"Romeo and Juliet" a Sweet Sorrow', *The Boston Globe*, 16 August: 67.

Engstrom, John (1985), 'A Fresh Look at Bard's "Comedy"', *The Boston Globe*, 7 August: 73.

Epstein, Jonathan (2021), 'Interview', 30 July.

Epstein, Jonathan (2022a), 'Interview', 28 February.

Epstein, Jonathan (2022b), 'Interview', 1 March.

Epstein, Jonathan (2023a), 'Email', 19 January.

Epstein, Jonathan (2023b), 'Email', 2 February.

Erickson, Peter (1981), 'A *Tempest* at The Mount', *Shakespeare Quarterly*, 32 (2): 188–90.

Fanger, Iris (1992), 'Director Returns to Her First Love', *Boston Herald*, 10 January, S19.

Fanger, Iris (1996), 'Review: Merry Wives of Windsor', *Boston Herald*, 15 August: 50.

Fanger, Iris (1997), 'Review: Henry IV, Part 1', *Boston Herald*, 19 August: 36.

Fanger, Iris (2005), *Patriot Ledger*, 1 August: 20.

Fox, Terry Curtis (1980), 'A Magic Mount', *The Village Voice*, 10–16 September: 10.

Friedman, Arthur (1992), 'Shirley Valentine Takes Audience on Charming Ride', 16 January: 51.

Fugle, Susie (2022), 'Interview', 24 August.

Gaber, Marjorie (2004), *Shakespeare after All*, 283, New York: Pantheon Books.

Gandolfi, Michael (2022), 'Interview', 2 September.

Gantz, Jeffrey (2015), '"Henry VI, Part 2" Comes to Life in Spirited Affair', *The Boston Globe*, 18 May: G5.

Garver, Krista (2022), 'Titus at Portland Playhouse', *Broadway World*, 25 March: 10.

Gates, Joanne E. (1981), 'Review of *The Tempest* at Shakespeare and Company', *Theatre Journal*, 33 (1): 116–17.
Gehman, Geoff (1989), '*As You Like It* by Tina Packer', *Shakespeare Bulletin*, 7 (2): 19–20.
Gelber, David (2020), 'Email', 10 November.
Goddard, Harold C. (1951), *The Meaning of Shakespeare*, Chicago: University of Chicago Press.
Gordon, Ronni (1988), *The Republican*, 13 July: 41.
Gordon, Ronni (2001), *The Republican*, 26 August: D1.
Gover, Tzivia, ed. (1998), '"Merchant" Raises Issues of Anti-Semitism', *Daily Hampshire Gazette*, 3 August: 7.
Greenblatt, Stephen (2008a), ' *A Midsummer Night's Dream,* Ed. and Intro.', in S. Greenblatt, W. Cohen, J. E. Howard and K. E. Maus (eds), *The Norton Shakespeare*, 839–96, New York: Norton.
Greenblatt, Stephen (2008b), '*Macbeth,* ed. and Intro.', in S. Greenblatt, W. Cohen, J. E. Howard, and K. E. Maus (eds), *The Norton Shakespeare*, 2569–632, New York: Norton.
Greenblatt, Stephen (2008c), 'Introduction to King Lear', in S. Greenblatt, W. Cohen, J. E. Howard and K. E. Maus (eds), *The Norton Shakespeare*, 2325–32, New York: Norton.
Griffin-Pressley, Deaon (2021), 'Interview', 27 December.
Gussow, Mel (1986), 'Outdoor "Antony"', *New York Times*, 24 July: C18.
Hadden, John (2021), 'Interview', 29 December.
Hadden, John (2022), 'Interview', 19 December.
Hadden, John (2023), 'Email', 6 December.
Hageman, Elizabeth H. (1984), 'Shakespeare in Massachusetts', *Shakespeare Quarterly*, 35 (2): 222–5.
Hammond, Michael (2022), 'Interview', 17 March.
Haring, Andrea (2022), 'Interview', 2 February.
Henderson, Diana (1995), 'Much Ado about Nothing by Tina Packer', *Shakespeare Bulletin*, 13 (4): 16.
Herodotus (1920), *The Histories* with an English translation by A. D. Godley, Cambridge, MA: Harvard University Press.
Hickey, Tamara (2021), 'Interview', 22 November.
Hill, Errol G. (1984a), 'Caliban and Ariel: A Study in Black and White in American Productions of The Tempest from 1945–1981', *Theatre History Studies*, 4: 1–10.
Hill, Errol G. (1984b), *Shakespeare in Sable: A History of Black Shakespearean Actors*, Amherst: The University of Massachusetts Press.

Holden, Stephen (1984), 'A "Dream" Outdoors', *The New York Times*, 6 September: C24.
Horne, Cloteal (2022), 'Interview', 27 April.
Isaac, Shahar (2022), 'Interview', 10 January.
Kaplan, M. Lindsay, ed. (2002), *The Merchant of Venice*, W. Shakespeare, Boston and New York: Bedford/St. Martin's.
Kelly, Kevin (1981), 'The Bard as You Like Him' *Boston Globe*, 16 July: 49–51.
Kelly, Kevin (1989), '"Tempest" Enchants, Despite Gregorys"', *Boston Globe*, 11 July: 55.
Kelly, Kevin (1993), 'A scorching Take on "Julius Caesar"', *Boston Globe*, 4 August: 67.
Kennedy, Louise (2005), *The Boston Globe*, 3 August: C5.
Kennedy, Louise (2007), *The Boston Globe*, 6 August: C4.
King, John (1989), 'City Lights Finds Show Biz Demanding', *The Boston Globe*, 18 July: 31.
Ko, Yu Jin (2008), 'Shakespeare in New England, 2007', *Shakespeare Bulletin*, 26 (1): 161–74.
Koblenz, Eleanor (1999), *The Daily Gazette*, 26 July: C7.
Levy, Daniel (2022), 'Interview', 7 March.
Levy, Daniel (2023), 'Email', 9 September.
Linklater, Kristin (2006), *Freeing the Natural Voice*, Hollywood, CA: Quite Specific Media Group, Ltd.
Littlefield, Thomson H. (1981), 'Shakespeare in Upstate New York', *Shakespeare Quarterly*, 32 (2): 187–8.
Littlefield, Thomson H. and Hugh Maclean (1980), 'Shakespeare in Upstate New York and Western New England', *Shakespeare Quarterly*, 31 (2): 181–4.
LoMonaco, Martha (2006), 'Regional/Resident Theatre', in Don B. Wilmeth and Christopher Bigsby (eds), *The Cambridge History of American Theatre*, vol. III, 224–48, Cambridge: Cambridge University Press.
Loomba, Ania (2006), 'Forward', in Ayanna Thompson (ed.), *Colorblind Shakespeare*, xiii–xvii, New York: Routledge.
MacDonald, Ronald R. (1986), 'Shakespeare in the Berkshires, 1985', *Shakespeare Quarterly*, 37 (1): 108–11.
Macon, Peter J. (2022), 'Interview', 11 March.
Massie, Raphael (2022), 'Interview', 21 June.
Maus, Katharine Eisaman (2008), 'Intro. and ed., *Julius Caesar*', in *The Norton Shakespeare*, 1549-1613, New York and London: W.W. Norton & Co.

McCleary, Dan (2022), 'Interview', 14 February.
Mento, Joan (1996), 'Review of "Measure for Measure" by Tina Packer', *Shakespeare Bulletin*, 14 (4): 18.
Mento, Joan (1998), 'Review of "The Merchant of Venice" by Tina Packer', *Shakespeare Bulletin*, 16 (4): 17–18.
Mento, Joan (2002), 'Review of "Macbeth" by Tina Packer', *Shakespeare Bulletin*, 20 (4): 16–17.
Mento, Joan (2006), 'Review of "King John" by Tina Packer', *Shakespeare Bulletin*, 24: 125–8.
Merlin, Bella (2021), 'Interview', 20 December.
Merlin, Bella and Tina Packer (2020), *Shakespeare & Company: When Action is Eloquence*, New York: Routledge.
Millonzi, Susannah (2022), 'Interview', 19 March.
Morton, Joe (2022), 'Interview', 11 March.
Nakamura, Midori (2022), 'Interview', 3 February.
Oliver, Arthur (2022a), 'Interview', 15 February.
Oliver, Arthur (2022b), 'Email', 4 April.
Oliver, Arthur (2022c), 'Email', 18 April.
Oliver, Arthur (2022d), 'Email', 10 August.
Oliver, Arthur (2023), 'Email', 23 August.
Ortiz, Edward (2002), *The Berkshire Eagle*, 14 June: D3
Packer, Tina (2016), *Women of Will: The Remarkable Evolution of Shakespeare's Female Characters*, New York: Vintage Books.
Packer, Tina (2002), Director's Note on *Macbeth*.
Packer, Tina (2020a), 'Interview', 26 January.
Packer, Tina (2020b), 'Interview', 16 February.
Packer, Tina (2020c), 'Interview', 11 September.
Packer, Tina (2021a), 'Interview', 19 February.
Packer, Tina (2021b), 'Interview', 16 April.
Packer, Tina (2022), 'Interview', 18 September.
Packer, Tina (2023a), 'Phone Conversation', 24 August.
Packer, Tina (2023b), 'Email', 4 September.
Pincus Andrew, L. (1996), 'The Final Act in a Squabble', *New York Times*, 18 August: H5.
Poole, William (2004), 'False Play: Shakespeare and Chess', *Shakespeare Quarterly*, 55 (1): 50–70.
Power, Cormac (2008), *Presence in Play: A Critique of Theories of Presence in the Theatre*, New York and Amsterdam: Brill.
Purcell, Stephen (2023), comment on draft, 'Shakespeare in the Theatre: Tina Packer'.

Randolph, Tod (2021), 'Interview', 8 November.
Rich, Frank (1981), 'Critic's Notebook; A Short Day's Journey to Eugene O'Neill's Childhood Home', *New York Times*, 6 August: C15.
Rothstein, Edward (1998), *New York Times*, 31 August: E2.
Rozett, Martha Tuck (2000), '*Coriolanus* by Tina Packer', *Shakespeare Bulletin*, 18 (4): 23–4.
Rozett, Martha Tuck (2001), '*A Midsummer Night's Dream* by Tina Packer', *Shakespeare Bulletin*, 19 (4): 20–1.
Saccio, Peter (1980), 'American Shakespeare Theatre, Stratford, Connecticut', *Shakespeare Quarterly*, 31 (2): 187–91.
Salsbury, Judy (1979), 'Shakespeare at "The Mount"', *Shakespeare Bulletin*, 30 (2): 177–8.
Sanders, Vicki (2006), 'Hauntingly Powerful "Hamlet"', *Boston Herald*, 12 July: 39.
Santa Rita, Michael (2002), *The Daily Gazette*, 21 June: D4.
Shapiro, James ([1996] 2016), *Shakespeare and the Jews*, New York: Columbia University Press.
Shepard, Richard F. (1982), 'Going out Guide', *New York Times*, 7 July: C16.
Siegel, Ed (1996), 'Full-bawdied "Measure" comes east', *Boston Globe*, 12 September: E2.
Siegel, Ed (1997), *Boston Globe*, 19 August: C4.
Siegel, Ed (1998), *Boston Globe*, 5 August: C8.
Siegel, Ed (1999), 'Packer's "Richard III" Considers the Women', *Boston Globe*, 15 July: E8.
Siegel, Ed (2002a), *Boston Globe*, 26 June: B2.
Siegel, Ed (2002b), *Boston Globe*, 28 July: L3.
Simotes, Tony (2002), 'Program Note'.
Simotes, Tony (2021), 'Interview', 20 December.
Sisto, Rocco (2022), 'Interview', 2 March.
Smith, Kiki (2021), 'Interview', 22 November.
Sokol, Fred (1999), '"Richard III" a Distinctive, Decisive Effort', *The Republican*, 22 July: D13.
Sokol, Fred (2002), *The Republican*, 25 July: D17.
Sokol, Fred (2003), 'Inspiring "King Lear" at Lenox Theater', 21 August: F14.
Taviani, F. (2005), 'Barba, Eugenio, and Nicola Savarese, *A Dictionary of Theatre Anthropology: The Secret Art of the Performer*, Taylor & Francis Group', *ProQuest Ebook Central*.

Available online http://ebookcentral.proquest.com/lib/csicuny/detail.action?docID=668433. Created from csicuny on 23 July 2023 18:48:25: 72.

Taylor, Markland (1988), 'Karen Allen is "As You Like It"', *New Haven Register*, 17 July: 10.

Thompson, Ayanna (2006), *Colorblind Casting*, New York and London: Routledge.

Turan, Kenneth (1985), 'Pillow Talk: Karen Allen', *Film Comment*, 21 (2): 34.

Tynan, Trudy (2001), *Associated Press*, 15 August: E1.

Walker, James (1994), 'Appendix', in Roger Warren and Stanley Wells (eds), *The Oxford Shakespeare: Twelfth Night* (1998): 222–36, Oxford: Oxford University Press, 1998.

Wilson, Walton (2022a), 'Interview', 22 February.

Wilson, Walton (2022b), 'Email', 29 November.

Wold, Kristin (2021), 'Interview', 5 November.

Wold, Kristin (2022), 'Interview', 25 February.

Yates, Frances (1966), *The Art of Memory*, London: Routledge and Keegan Paul.

Youngerman, Jim (2022), 'Interview', 25 August.

INDEX

Abbruzzese, Kate 160, 161
All's Well That Ends Well (2008 production) 129
Allen, Karen 56–8, 60, 62, 68, 70
Anderson, Susan Heller 40
Antony and Cleopatra (1986 production) 51–2
Arendt, Hanna 11, 165
Arnold, Trish 13
As You Like It (productions)
 1981 39
 1988 20, 55–69
 1990 70
Aspenlieder, Elizabeth 99–100
Asprey, Martin J. 83, 85, 86, 100, 101, 107, 111, 116, 125, 141
Aucoin, Dan 130

Ballou, Bill 25, 32, 33
Barba, Eugenio 4
Barclay, Bill 117
Barge, Gillian 23, 29, 30
Barnes, Clive 165
Barry, B. H. 13, 28–30, 39
Barton, John 13, 14
Bass, Milton R. 34, 115
Bassi, Shaul 133
Beaumont, Karen 85
Bennett, Fran 50–1
Bentley, Kenajuan 124
Berek, Peter 39, 41, 48, 49

Berenson, Mitch 15, 17
Bergman, Peter J. 166
Best, Martin 117
Black National Theatre of Harlem 2
Block, Larry 45
Bock, Ariel 78, 96, 98, 99
Booth, Eric 30
Borak, Jeffrey 57, 69, 116, 121, 126, 143, 165
Boston Shakespeare Company 21, 50, 62
Brantley, Ben 55, 72, 77, 78, 80, 119, 125, 126
Brazzle, Thomas 151, 157, 159–63
breath
 beginning again 89
 connection to body, sound, voice, and psyche 8, 12, 139
 and creativity 7, 8
Breithbarth, David 38
Brook, Peter 14, 78
Broome, John 13, 28, 29, 39
Brown, Pamela 78
Burrows, Allyn 19, 79, 80, 83, 84, 86–8, 100–1, 117–20, 125
Byrd, Deborah Ann 166
Byrne Terry 81, 82, 94, 98, 110, 113, 116

C., R. 40, 44, 47
Calhoun, Kaia 29, 30, 39–41, 43, 44, 46
Carr, Jay 52
Cartelli, Thomas 49
casting
  and change 3
  colourblind 1, 2
  multiple 1, 55, 56, 76
  multicultural 2, 52, 54, 56, 91, 127
    The Comedy of Errors 50, 51
    Measure for Measure 81
    The Merchant of Venice 131, 137, 146, 150, 151
    Romeo and Juliet 2
    The Tempest 36–7, 69
    Twelfth Night 39, 47, 49
Ciulei, Liviu 46
Clarke, Henry David 107, 111
Clay, Carolyn 66
Clayton, Thomas 47
clown 14
  As You Like It (1988)
    Celia 60–2;
    Le Beau 66–9
  Commedia dell'arte 14
  the drop 43, 45, 104, 182 n.3
  The Tempest (1980) 36
  Twelfth Night (1981–2) 39, 41, 43, 46
Cobb, Mel 98, 118, 119
Coffin, David 40, 41
Cohen, Walter 182–3 n.7

Cole, Gregory Uel 14, 26, 27, 29, 30, 37, 39, 46, 48
Coleman, Kevin 14, 29, 38, 46, 47, 49, 74–6, 89, 97, 116
Comedy of Errors, The (productions)
  1983 49, 50
  1984 51
  1985 51
Conway, Merry 14, 39, 46
Cook, Amy 3
Corfman, Caris 32
Coriolanus (productions)
  2000 94
  2001 93, 94
  2007 126
Crew, Bob 48
Croy, Jonathan 155
Cymbeline (2017 production) 130, 166

Daniels, James Robert 72
Davenport, Johnny Lee 83, 85, 86, 89, 111
Davis, Herb 38
Dench, Judi 18
Derakhshani, Tirdad 166
Dibble, Susan 14, 58, 72, 101, 136, 155
Dolan, Frances 164
Douglas, Timothy 59, 60, 66–9
dropping in 3, 5–9, 24, 26, 29, 34, 37, 41, 43, 47, 58, 66, 73, 82, 84, 120–1, 123, 140, 142, 149, 153–5, 159–60, 166
Duckett, Richard 129
Dunning, Jennifer 40, 41

Eck, Michael 78, 90, 114, 125, 141, 146
Eckert, Thor, Jr. 31, 33, 36
Edith Wharton Restoration, Inc. 17, 80, 93, 97
Egozi, Noah 151
Elizabethan Theatre
training for 13
energy
  and the actors' art 3, 6–8, 11, 140, 151–3, 166
  and the actors' presence 4
  and audience reception 3, 5, 11, 42–3, 47, 58, 67, 75, 116
  as central to the theatrical experience 11
  and collaborative play 4, 5, 75, 152
  definition and modes of acting 3, 4
  as magic in *Macbeth* 108–9
  and theatre space 114
  when playing multiple roles 83, 151
Engstrom, John 49–51
Epstein, Jonathan 53, 57–60, 62–6, 71–8, 80, 90, 93–5, 97, 98, 102–4, 131–3, 135, 137–9, 142–6, 156–8, 165
Erickson, Peter 31–6, 38

Fanger, Iris 70, 80, 90, 117, 125
Feldenkrais, Moshé 14
fight, as storytelling 90, 91, 99, 112–13
Fingerhut, Arden 57
Five College Consortium 28

Fletcher, Rachel 55
Ford Foundation 12–14, 28
Fox, Terry Curtis 36, 37
Freedom Theatre of Philadelphia 2
Freeman, Neil 39, 44, 58
Friedman, Arthur 70
Fugle, Susie 26–8, 30

Gandolfi, Michael 102
Gantz, Jeffrey 130
Garver, Krista 166
Gates, Joanne E. 32, 35–7
Gates, Samuel R. 99
Gehman, Geoff 56, 69
Gelber, David 165
Goddard, Harold C. 29
Gordon, Ronni 62, 95
Gore, Nigel 126, 130
Gover, Tzivia 131–3
Greenblatt, Stephen 182 n.5, 182 n.7
Gregory, André 69
Gregory, Marina 69
Griffin-Pressley, Deaon 9, 151, 159, 161–3, 166
Gussow Mel 52

Hadden, John 26–8, 41–4, 50, 148, 149, 152, 157, 164
Hageman, Elizabeth H. 50
Hammond, Michael 30, 50, 107, 110, 111, 114, 115
Haring, Andrea 24, 25, 27
Heilbron, Lorna 29, 30
Henderson, Diana 78, 79
Henry IV, Part 1 (1997 production) 89

Henry V1, Part 2: The Contention (Productions)
2015 130
2023 1, 167
Henry VIII (2013 production) 130
Herodotus 113–14
Hickey, Tamara 155–8, 164
Hill, Errol G. 50
Holden, Stephen 50
Holdridge, Eleanor 93, 126
Horne, Cloteal 9, 149, 151, 159, 161
Huang, Mark 114
Hynek, Robin 83

Ingram, Elizabeth 129
Ingram, Malcolm 76, 77, 116, 137, 139
Isaac, Shahar 147, 150, 151, 153, 154, 164
Israel, Jennie 107, 111

Johnson, Gregory 39
Julius Caesar (Productions)
1992–3 20, 56, 70–8, 98
2014 130

Kapp, Richard 13, 15
Kelly, Kevin 40, 44, 69–72, 76, 77
Kennedy, Louise 121, 125, 126
King John (2005 production) 20, 94, 116–25
King Lear (2003 production) 94, 116–17
Koblenz, Eleanor 94

Kol Nidre 131, 135, 145–6, 164–5, 183–4 n.5
Krausnick, Dennis 14, 17, 23, 26, 29, 30, 49, 125
Kunis, Tom 38

Learned Ladies, The (1978 production) 14
Leavis, F. R. 16
Levy, Daniel 148–50, 165
Linklater, Kristin 12–14, 26, 28, 29, 39, 40, 43, 45, 46, 53, 58, 60
Littlefield, T. H. 30
LoMonaco, Martha 168
London Academy of Music and Drama (LAMDA) 12, 15
Loomba, Ania 3
Lowry, McNeil 14

Macbeth (productions)
1982 49, 51, 53, 54
2002 20, 94, 106–17
McCleary, Dan 108–14, 141
MacDonald, Karen 70
MacDonald, Ronald R. 51
Mackintosh, Iain 18
Maclean, Hugh 30
Macon, Peter 9, 118–22
McSpadden, Judith 111
Marcell, Joseph (Joe) 2, 30
Marsh, George E. Jr. 18
Massie, Paul 45
Massie, Raphael 151, 154, 159, 163, 164
Maus, Katharine Eisaman 76, 77
May, Corinna 14, 78, 91

Measure for Measure (1996 production) 20, 55, 56, 80–9
Mento, Joan 83, 84, 86, 88, 89, 113, 118, 120, 127, 135, 142, 146
Merchant of Venice, The (productions)
  1998 20, 93, 130–47
  2016 20, 127, 130, 131, 147–65
Merlin, Bella 12–16, 22, 53, 152, 154
Merry Wives of Windsor (1995 production) 80–1
A Midsummer Night's Dream (productions)
  1978 20, 22–30
  1984 49–50
  1993 78
  2001 93, 95–105
Miller, Annette 117, 140, 141
Miller, Mike 17
Miller Building 18
Millonzi, Susannah 117, 121–4
Moran, Dan 50
Morton, Joe 22, 33–7
Much Ado About Nothing (production 1995) 78–80, 91
multicultural 2, 3, 16, 20, 22, 30, 39, 51, 52, 54, 56, 127, 131, 137, 146, 151, 154, 159, 163

Nakamura, Midori 60–2, 68, 69, 91
Ness, Virginia 39, 40, 42, 46
New York University 14, 26, 28, 46

Oberlin, Richard 52
Odland, Bruce 40, 45, 56, 58
Ohama, Natsuko 2, 27
Oliver, Arthur 99, 100, 103, 117, 118, 136, 137
O'Neill, Eugene 54
O'Neill Center 13
Ortiz, Edward 109, 112

Packer, Tina
  as actor 12, 70, 80, 125–6, 129, 165, 166
  as artistic director 31, 129
  as author 126, 129, 178 n.1
  as director
    on multicultural casting 2, 3
    on Shakespeare's plays 4
    philosophy of theatre 2, 3, 12, 96
    styles of staging
      background movement 52, 80
      bare bard 19, 55, 70–90
      dumb shows 117
      grand mise en scène 19, 40, 53, 55, 70, 90, 130, 135
      immersive 20, 32, 79, 80
      playhouse style 19, 126, 130
      use of stage floor 107, 117, 118, 126–7
    work with individual actors 59–70
Papp, Joseph 22
Performing Garage (NYC) 13
Pennoyer, John 71, 90

Pericles (2010 production) 129
Pincus Andrew L. 81
Poole, William 183 n.8
Pratt, Noni 27
Primus, Barry 30
Prospect Park, Brooklyn 39, 40

Randelman, Garfield 38
Randolph, Tod 71, 72, 76, 77, 135, 137, 139–44
Ransom, Kenneth 19, 69, 78, 91
Reeves, Keanu 69
regional theatre 13, 167, 168
rehearsal
  dropping in 6–10, 41, 43
  improvisation 26, 29, 41, 58–60
  movement exercises 10, 138, 139
  Packer's process 5–11
  stumble through 10
  stagger through 10
Reidy, Clare 123
Reynolds, Roger 32, 33
Rhoades, Tori 137
Rich, Frank 54
Richard III (productions)
  1999 94
  2012 130
Roberts, Carolyn 109, 111, 114
Romeo and Juliet (productions)
  1979 2, 30, 54
  1984 49, 51
Rothstein, Edward 132, 133, 146
Royal Academy of Dramatic Art (RADA) 11
Rozett, Martha Tuck 94, 98–104, 127
Rutledge, Jonathan 27

Saccio, Peter 181 n.3
Salsbury, Judy 23, 25, 26, 28
Sanders, Vicki 126
Santa Rita, Michael 115
Saukiavicus, Timothy 49
Sellars, Peter 21
Shakespeare & Company
  Founding 11–17
  Kemble Street Theatres
    Arthur S. Waldstein Amphitheatre 18
    Elayne Bernstein Performing Arts Building 18
    Founders' Theatre (renamed Tina Packer Playhouse) 18
    Roman Garden Theatre 18
    Rose Footprint Theatre, The 18
  The Mount Theatres
    mainstage (outdoor amphitheatre) 22, 55
    The Salon 17, 55
    Stables Theatre 19, 55
  move to Kemble St., Lenox 17
  organization 18–19
Shakespeare Theatre Association 167
Shapiro, James 131, 133, 138
Shay, Michelle 52

Shepard, Richard F. 39
Siegel, Ed 81, 82, 94, 109, 115, 144, 146
Simotes, Tony 14, 26, 27, 29, 99, 100, 112
Sims, Barbara 117
Sims, Neil 35–6
Sisto, Rocco 29, 30, 36, 41, 42, 44–6, 48, 69, 91
Skelton, Ty 137
Smith, Kiki 25, 34, 69
Smith College 14–15
Sokol, Fred 94, 109, 115, 116

Taming of the Shrew, The (1973 production) 13, 14
Taviani, F. 3, 4
Taylor, Markland 57, 62, 65
Tempest, The (productions)
  1980 20, 22, 31–9, 54, 103
  1989 69–70, 91
Thompson, Ayanna 178–9 n.2
Thompson, John Douglas 53, 78, 91, 135, 139–41
Titus Andronicus (2022 production) 167
Toomey, Michael 137
Toussant, Lorraine 49, 53
Troilus and Cressida (2012 production) 130
Turan, Kenneth 56

Twelfth Night (1981/1982 productions) 20, 22, 39–49, 54
Tynan, Trudy 95, 97

Varga, Brian 38
Villanueva, Kristin 129

Walker, James 40
Ware, Jenna 137
Warren, Iris 12
Weiss, Gina 27
Wharton, Edith 16–18
Wilson Walton 81, 85, 86, 120, 121
Winter's Tale, The (1979 production) 3, 31, 98
Wold, Kristin 79, 80, 84, 87–9, 155
words
  and the actors' emotions 8
  compared to musical notes 15
  and the creation of identity 11
  dropping in 7–9, 166
  Kol Nidre 165
  language as experience 2, 56

Yates, Frances 147
Youngerman, Jim 95, 103
Yulin, Harris 22, 32, 37–9

www.ingramcontent.com/pod-product-compliance
Lightning Source LLC
Chambersburg PA
CBHW052113300426
44116CB00010B/1658